Jesus
ON STAGE

John's Gospel and Greek Tragedy

Philip Oakeshott

author**HOUSE**®

AuthorHouse™ UK
1663 Liberty Drive
Bloomington, IN 47403 USA
www.authorhouse.co.uk
Phone: 0800 047 8203 (Domestic TFN)
*   +44 1908 723714 (International)*

Published by AuthorHouse 12/26/2019

ISBN: 978-1-7283-9738-2 (sc)
ISBN: 978-1-7283-9737-5 (e)

Print information available on the last page.

This book is printed on acid-free paper.

Greek Bible text from: Novum Testamentum Graece, 28th revised edition, Edited by Barbara Aland and others, © 2012 Deutsche Bibelgesellschaft, Stuttgart.

Jesus
ON STAGE

Acknowledgements

All translations from Greek and Latin in this book are mine, working from the Aland New Testament (4th rev. ed.), and from the classical texts of the Loeb Classical Library. All or most Bible translations, and even occasionally the Loeb translations, at times conceal some aspect of the truth; for example, the stage-directions added to the text of a play represent only an individual editor's, sometimes outmoded, perception of the ways in which such plays were produced. As translator, my wording cannot help but coincide often with that of other translators, to whom indeed I owe a great deal; but my only conscious plagiarism is of E.V. Rieu's **'pitched his tent among us'** (John 1.14).

I wish to express my warmest appreciation of good advice and encouragement given during the earliest stages of my studies in the gospel of John and of the classic and the Hellenistic Greek drama by my late friend Keith Treacher, the late Henry Chadwick, Professor Paul Anderson of George Fox University, Washington, and Professor Howard Jacobson of Illinois University, none of whom are to be held responsible for the ideas expressed in this book, still less for any errors which it may contain.

Once more I must thank Southampton University for allowing me the use of their library, and Southampton Central Library for their unflagging zeal in finding me books from other libraries all over Britain.

My special thanks to Canon John Davies, formerly Lecturer in New Testament Studies at Southampton University, whose friendship has always rendered his very pertinent criticisms not merely acceptable but enjoyable; and also to my resident computer expert, without whose unfailing help this book could not have been written.

Contents

Introduction

In *The Man that Peter Knew* I argued that Mark's Gospel was an honest, if at times imperfect account of Jesus' ministry, and still our best source for Jesus' life. *Greek Tragedy and the Gospel of John* is, on the other hand, intended to show that factual biography was not at any point the Fourth Evangelist's intention.

John[1], almost certainly published between 90 and 115 AD, has been a puzzle from the beginning, being so obviously different from the already established Synoptic gospels (i.e., Mark, Matthew and Luke) in its storyline, its teaching, and its portrayal of Jesus himself. The earliest evaluation we have of this gospel, by the scholar Clement of Alexandria, writing little more than a century after John's likely date of publication, stated flatly that '**John, the very last** (of the evangelists)**, realising that the physical facts** *(ta somatika)* **had been set out clearly in the** (earlier) **gospels, urged by his friends and inspired by the spirit** *(pneumati)*, **created a spiritual gospel** *(pneumatikon poiēsai euaggelion)*.'[2] The implication is clear; and although the church came to treat this gospel as factual, we should not today overlook Clement's distinction between the known, physical facts concerning Jesus, recorded by the first three evangelists, and this inspired, but much less factual gospel which the fourth evangelist composed. (*Poieō* is the word used for all creative work, be it poetry, drama or sculpture, or the God of Genesis creating the world; *graphō*, to write, is what they say of Mark.) Certainly, whoever composed it, the Fourth Gospel has a theological depth undreamed of among its predecessors; but also, as Clement quite clearly says, it is primarily concerned with the theological significance of the principal facts in the Synoptic record – the preaching and teaching, the healings, the crucifixion and the resurrection; and, as I will add, wherever an invented incident will best suit his purpose, the fourth evangelist creates one.

The thesis set out in this book is that the first draft of the Gospel of John was intended to be a stage-play for the Greek theatre, imitating those of Aeschylus, Sophocles or Euripides, the great classical dramatists of the fifth century BC; and based, loosely, on the events of Passion Week. Later, however, the author changed direction and expanded that draft into a Greek historical novel or 'romance', a genre which flourished from perhaps the first century BC at least until the third century AD. At both stages, then, a work of fiction; of historical fiction, insofar as it deals with a historical person, but not in the sense of trying to present an accurate historical account of that person and the events of his life. Like Shakespeare, painting Richard III as a complete villain coming to disaster or Henry V as the triumphant ideal king, the evangelist depicts his Jesus as God in human form, with supernatural power and insight, yet submitting calmly to a dreadful fate and so achieving the greatest of all victories. John is trying to express what he sees as the significant truth about Jesus through the medium of historical fiction.

It is in this gospel that Pontius Pilate asks, as the story reaches its crisis, 'What is truth?' 'All Truth is a shadow, except the last, except the utmost; *yet every Truth is true in its kind*', says Isaac Pennington, an early Quaker (italics mine). What *kind* of truth is John putting forward? Fiction or drama based on history can have its own validity – consider, for example, T.S. Eliot's *Murder in the Cathedral*.

John himself makes his approach quite clear with a prologue outlining his theological view of Jesus as the Incarnate Word of God; and reinforces it at the end of his main book when, after saying that there were many other 'signs' which Jesus did and the disciples witnessed, '**not recorded in this book**' he continues: '**But those written here have been recorded *so that you may believe that Jesus is the Christ, the Son of God,* and that through this faith you may possess eternal life by means of his name**' (John 20.30-31). Unlike Mark, John abandons accurate biography in favour of a very dramatic theological interpretation of Jesus. This gospel is often inspired and inspiring fiction, a store of many treasures; but it will become all the more valuable once we have recognized that historical fact was never the author's concern: the truth he sought to express was of another kind, expressed through a different medium.

1

A Historical Novel

As in an archaeological excavation, this enquiry must chart the topmost layer of the site before digging deeper: we must survey the narrative gospel as it is now found in the New Testament before we can begin to examine its possible dramatic content. The first stage is to examine the present text to see whether it supports my prime contention that the fourth gospel is a work of fiction; a work now of historical fiction, and resembling in that respect other books that can be found in the Old Testament and the Apocrypha (see below). Only then shall we be ready to delve deeper for traces of an earlier version.

The Fictional Element in John

If one tried to write a novel about Jesus, it might not be long before one found oneself turning more and more to John for lively incident, dramatic tension, or the mechanics of plot; and the suspicion might finally dawn that the evangelist had himself written just such a novel. Once that thought occurs, the evidence is not far to seek.

John has long been acknowledged as a remarkable piece of writing, with even C.H. Dodd (1963 p.18), the most convinced twentieth century champion of this gospel's historical value, remarking that it was **'to a degree unequalled by the other gospels, an original literary composition'**. Many scholars have held that the fourth evangelist drew on a tradition independent of that of the Synoptic gospels. Opinions vary from Dodd's claims for the high factual content of John's tradition to A.T. Hanson's view that it was inferior; but most scholars support the independence of John and many -- C.K. Barrett is a notable exception -- deny him any knowledge of Mark. Yet, apart from any conscious, or possibly subconscious, wish to uphold John as true witness, the idea that it is historically valuable rests mainly on the assumption that it at least purports to be an attempt at history. When Stibbe (1992, p.74) says that **'Historians like Mark and John do not invent details in order to create a sense of factuality'**, this may be true of historians in general and of Mark in particular; but it begs the question about John. Perhaps the author was *not* a historian? Stibbe talks of **'fictionalized history'**, but writers of fiction, however historical, invariably do add detail, for verisimilitude and for greater interest. This study will maintain that the fourth evangelist draws on the Synoptics, and possibly on Paul as well, radically reshaping their words for reasons which are sometimes theological but as often artistic; with some passages drawing on the practice of his church or the knowledge of its members; and that the clear differences and discrepancies between his narrative and the Synoptic ones is due, not to knowledge of some other tradition, but to his ruthless adaption of the synoptic one for his own medium -- fiction.

The Ancient Novel

C.S. Lewis once attempted a black-and-white dismissal of the possibility that John could be anything other than the recording of fact:

> **'Of this text there are only two possible views. Either this is reportage -- though no doubt it may contain errors -- pretty close to the facts; nearly as close as Boswell. Or else, some unknown writer in the second century, without known predecessors or successors, suddenly anticipated the whole technique of modern, novelistic, realistic narrative. If it is untrue, it must be narrative of that kind. The reader who doesn't see this simply has not learned to read.'[3]**

Lewis' literary judgement here may well be sound; more so perhaps than the recent tendency to classify John as a *bios,* for although the book can be said to have the form of Greek popular biography, the writer's inventiveness, ruthless reshaping of sources, and above all sophistication of plot, so different from the almost unconnected episodes which make up, say, a *bios* like the *Life of Aesop,* all identify the gospel as a novel. Lewis's mistake was to suppose that the gospel's author would have *needed* to anticipate the technique of the historical novel, which was already flourishing in the Graeco-Roman world; 'John' had many predecessors and successors in that genre. The gospel may seem 'modern' and 'realistic' because of the author's talent for lively dialogue,[4] which is indeed livelier than that of most ancient novels, but lively dialogue has always been, as both Old Testament and Apocrypha can show, a notable characteristic of Jewish and Graeco-Jewish storytelling; but, like these, John also contains much that is neither realistic nor, as serious history, very plausible.

A great deal of fiction was written in the Hellenistic period which followed Alexander's conquests and the early centuries of the Roman empire which followed it, owing partly to the increase in literacy and perhaps also to a new individualism as people strove to find purpose and identity in the enormous world of empire (Perry, pp.78, 140). Those novels which have survived can reasonably be dated as early as the first century BC or as late as the third century AD, and their production was rising towards a peak at the beginning of the second century AD (Reardon, 1989, p.5), which is a likely time for John's gospel to have been written. Whatever the causes, there was a market for fiction, varying from a high-minded Utopia like Iambulus' *Island of the Sun* to the bawdy *Milesian Tales* of Aristides, but including also genuine 'romances', novels like Chariton's *Chaereas and Callirhoe*, the *Ninus Romance* and *The Dream of Nectanebus*.[5]

Often such novels made some use of known historical characters; but, like modern ones, they varied, from those telling a romantic story with minimal factual content to those like *The Alexander Romance*, **'a narrative about a historical figure, with a historical basis but with much additional material casting light on the hero's significance and making the story more exciting'**.[6] That phrase aptly describes the type of historical novel which is sometimes mistaken for a popular biography; and it is to this ambivalent genre that John properly belongs.

The Jewish Greek novella

The Jewish people have always been much given to storytelling, an art form that breaks neither the second nor the fourth commandment. There was no language barrier between the majority of Jews and the Greek-speaking culture of the eastern Roman empire in which they lived. In Palestine itself (which had been under the rule of Alexander and his successors for longer than India was ever held by the British) Greek was much spoken, and a great many Jews lived in Greek-speaking cities abroad. So novels in Greek were written also by Jews. The Genesis-based love-story of *Joseph and Aseneth* is thought to be one of the oldest of the ancient 'romances'; and the fact that this whole passionate tale is spun from just two verses of Genesis (Ch.41.45,51), shows how far such a novel might be creative rather than historical.

The Hebrew scriptures already contained three early examples of the historical novella: *Jonah, Ruth* and *Esther. Jonah* is, like the Arthurian legends or the novels of William Morris, set in a vague past which allows for marvels; *Ruth* is a naturalistic and charming 'period' love-story; *Esther*, whose historical improbabilities culminate with a Persian monarch agreeing to the wholesale massacre by his Hebrew subjects of any of his other subjects who are their enemies (Esth.8.10 -- 9.16), is strong on background, suspense, drama and humour. Although these were not composed in Greek, anyone with a copy of the Septuagint would find Greek versions of *Ruth* and *Esther* in the histories and *Jonah* amongst the prophets.

The term 'novella' is applied by L.M. Wills to the Jewish tales in Greek, usually much shorter than the extensive

5

novels of Greek and Roman authors.[7] In this category he includes Daniel.1-6 (*'Adventures at the Persian court'*) with the related Daniel stories of *Susannah* and *Bel and the Dragon*; also *Tobit, Judith*, and *Esther*. Although culturally different from the Greek ones (more inhibited about sex, for example)[8] they show how longstanding was the Jewish tradition of writing fiction in Greek; and Erich Gruen (2002, pp.135-212) has shown how cavalierly they treated history and tradition, and how pervasive were the elements of humour and exaggeration. Whether the Christian author of John's 'gospel' was from a Jewish family or not, he might easily have turned to the Greek 'romance'genre.

Most of the Greek 'romances', says Perry, are what would today be called historical novels. In style the Greek novel '**was fundamentally drama in substance and historiography in its outward form**'. The author of John did not need to create a new art form, for this lay ready to his hand. Even if not himself a Jew, but moving in the Graeco-Jewish milieu of the Near Eastern church, he would have known these stories, and has displayed notable talent in creating, I suggest, a work in the same genre. Corroboration comes from the fact that, once viewed as a novelist, he can be seen to be using every type of novelistic technique, and some of the most obvious will now be considered.

Ubiquity and Omniscience.

The first indication that John is creative fiction is the writer's use of what novelists call the 'God's eye' view; he tells his story with complete knowledge of what is happening to different people in different places. For example, in the story of the Woman of Samaria (John 4.3-42), there is first a vivid dialogue between her and Jesus, in the explicit absence of the disciples; next, although the disciples are now back with Jesus at the well, we hear what the woman is saying to her neighbours in the town; and when these too have come and spoken to Jesus, we are told what they say to the woman when they go home again.

The healing of the Man Born Blind (John 9.1-41) and its subsequent controversies make this clearer still. Jesus spreads a paste of earth and spittle over the blind man's eyes and sends him to wash it off in the pool of Siloam. The narrative follows the man to the pool and describes his cure, then back to his home where his neighbours question him about his astonishing transformation. Then he is brought before the Pharisees, and there is a word-for-word report of their questioning. They summon the man's parents, and we hear what they say, too. The man is called back and, after more argument, expelled from the synagogue. Such a narrative bears all the signs of a creative author, trusting to a good story to carry the reader past minor implausibilities.[9]

Further, the writer not only knows what everyone says, but also what they think.[10] He is able to tell us what Jesus thought, and what he meant; what the disciples thought, what 'the Jews' thought, and even, it seems, what the devil had done to the thinking of Judas (John 13.2). More importantly, at all times the author can explain the significance of what is happening, which everyone else, except for Jesus, fails to understand. This has to be creative writing.

Documentary Sources

Another consideration is the author's use of sources, a much contested aspect of Johannine scholarship.[11] The strength of the case against the author's use of Mark rests on the fact that there are only a few stories in John which are closely related to Marcan ones, and these all show substantial differences. As long as the question asked is, did the fourth evangelist copy from Mark *in the same way that Matthew, and sometimes Luke, clearly did*, then the answer must be, No, he did not. His way with sources differed from theirs.

Wills shows very clearly a great correspondence between John and Mark, which he attributes to their both having, as their common source, a hypothetical popular biography, similar to *The Life of Aesop* (Wills 1997, pp.51-115). Mark, indeed, is stylistically similar to the series of fables with brief contexts, within a very sketchy plot, which make up the *bios* of Aesop; but John is a more subtle, more complex and better constructed story. What makes Wills' *bios* as irrelevant as the 'Signs' and 'Miracles' Gospels conjectured by earlier scholars as sources for John, is the simple fact that copying is not the method of a writer of fiction. Such authors will borrow names, places, incidents, phrases, even vocabulary, and use them with the greatest freedom to create a new narrative, specifically developed to attract and hold the interest of readers. To suggest that such a complex interweaving of strands from different traditions as is found in the Lazarus and the Anointing stories *could only have happened before those traditions had been written down* (Fortna 1970, pp.76, 84), is to underestimate creative writers in general, and this one in particular.

The Anointing at Bethany remains clearly the same story first recorded in Mark: as do the Feeding of the Crowd, Walking on the Water and Peter's Denial. Yet there are others in which the finished version is hardly recognisable as dependent in any way on a synoptic original: compare, for example, the healing of the paralytic in Mark 2.1-12 with the healing and completely different controversy in John 5.1-47. The unusual word *krabbaton* for the bed, which each paralytic obediently hoists onto his back and carries away, reveals the link; but the fourth evangelist has turned the incident into a very different story. The same is true of his Blind Man story, while his raising of Lazarus owes no more to the Synoptics than the basic idea of raising the dead.

Disregarding all conjectured sources unless and until proved necessary, the known writings available to the fourth evangelist would have been the synoptic gospels and some at least of the epistles of Paul. There is no *a priori* reason why, by the end of the first century, any flourishing city church around the Mediterranean should not have had its own copies of these, for by the time there was one Christian capable of writing John, there must have been many who had time and skill enough to copy a short book, or the money to pay a copyist;[12] while excellent communications around the empire made dissemination quick and easy. The preservation of Paul's letters proves the interest of the early church in the written word; while the evidence of Papias shows that Mark's gospel, at least, reached Asia Minor while one of Jesus' disciples was still alive there to review it (Eusebius, *EH* 3.39.15). During the latter half of the first century, as the eye-witnesses were dying out, written gospels would have become increasingly valued and widely distributed.

Despite many theories advanced for other sources,[13] the availability and use of known Christian writings remains the least speculative hypothesis. How, then, has the fourth evangelist employed these? Once his technique as novelist is properly understood there is no need to search beyond Mark, Luke and perhaps Matthew for the sources of John's narrative; but all of these have been adapted so freely that their use is seldom obvious.

How the Sources were Used

The creative author's hand is shown in the way that diverse elements are blended into neat, coherent narratives. The Man Brought Back to Life (perhaps originating from Luke's Young Man at Nain) is given the name of Lazarus, a dialect version of Eleazar, probably borrowed from the parable in Luke 17.19-31 whose the punch-line ends '**they will not believe, though one rose from the dead**'. His sisters become Martha and Mary, found in Luke 10.38-42, and they are placed conveniently at Bethany, where Mark had said that Jesus and the Twelve lodged before Passover. The writer twice uses Mark's verb *embrimaomai* (to be angry or upset: Mark 1.43; John 11.33, 38) to describe Jesus' emotions here. Both emotion and word were, I suggest, borrowed from Mark, together with *pistikos* for the unguent, to lend this episode an air of authenticity convincing to the reader – and sometimes, it seems, also to the critic. Mary now becomes the woman of Mark's anointing episode (Mark 14.3-9) and the anointing takes place in Lazarus' house, so editing out the irrelevant character of Simon the Leper.

Criticism of the woman's wastefulness is no longer from unspecified persons, but is assigned to Judas Iscariot, allowing the author to insert a second 'little cloud' to foreshadow later developments. (The first was John 6.70, '**one of you is a devil**'). These hints prepare us for the horror of Judas' treachery, the accusation here being that he was a thief and stole from the common purse. This baseless charge of dishonesty passes well enough in reading, but will not stand scrutiny, since it would hardly have been discovered after Judas' defection, nor passed over if detected before.

What our author is doing, quite rightly, is to shape an amorphous mass of synoptic episodes into something more coherent. The full array of gospel characters is slimmed down, but given greater individuality. Many minor characters are named, and some are used repeatedly, so that helpful Andrew, naive Philip and pessimistic Thomas act as 'tie-rods', to borrow a phrase which Dorothy Sayers used for the ones which she herself invented or developed for *The Man Born to be King* (a sequence of radio plays broadcast in 1941-2), like her Roman centurion 'Proclus' and Pilate's wife 'Claudia'. Just as Sayers used King Balthazar to link birth and crucifixion, so in John 'Nicodemus' is used to link the burial, closing the earthly ministry, to the earliest teaching at its start. Lesser characters are given at least a touch of individuality: the servant who lost his ear is 'Malchus', and now it was Peter who attacked him; the girl who challenges Peter is the doorkeeper, the last challenger is Malchus' cousin. It all adds verisimilitude.

It is precisely this very free, novelistic treatment of stories which has so often been explained by supposing that the author of John did not know the synoptic Gospels. W. Nicol (1972, p.3), objecting that, in those stories closest to the Synoptics, John agrees partly with one and partly with another, has in fact put his finger on the novelist's eclectic approach. D. Moody Smith (1995, p.63), who does not believe that the boy with the loaves and fishes would have been inserted by an author using the Marcan story *since to do so serves no theological purpose*, has failed to see that a creative writer might add the delightfully willing little boy simply to make the story more appealing, the detail of Philip consulting Andrew to make it more convincing. Writers of fiction do not *copy* their sources; they borrow and adapt, exactly as suits them.

Occasionally John follows a Marcan story so closely that it remains recognisable; notably, as C.K. Barrett points out,[14] with the Feeding of the Crowd and the Walking on Water stories (Mark 6.35-52; John 6.1-21) and later with Peter's Denial (Mark 14.54, 66-72; John 18.15-18, 25-27). Alternatively, the author will borrow a mere phrase or motif with which to build a whole new story: for example, in the Court Official's Son (John 4.43-54), *ho pais mou*, 'my boy', as ambiguous in Greek as it is in English, was used in Matthew 8.5-13 by the Centurion for 'my slave', and here by the author of John to mean 'my son'. The concept of healing an unseen patient is retained, but with details more dramatic and impressive.

Note, however, that the fourth evangelist has reversed here the emphasis of the original story. In Matthew, Jesus offers to go and heal the servant, and it is the centurion, in an astonishing display of trust, who refuses to let him come: '**just say the word, and my slave will be healed**'. In John, Jesus rejects the father's urgent plea to come to his son with a withering comment about lack of trust, and sends the father back alone as a test of his faith: '**March**', says Jesus, using the same verb that the centurion used to his soldiers (John 4.50; Matt.8.9).[15] This ruthless adapting of a source to the author's own ends would be typical creative writing.

Background and local colour.

Plausibility is a major concern for the historical novelist, modern or ancient, for readers have more leisure to be critical than the spectators at a play. **'It is frequently John who supplies the reason and meaning of actions and speeches that in the Synoptics appear unexplained and disconnected'** says Sayers, instancing the attempt to make Jesus a king as explaining why, after Feeding the Crowd, he hid himself and sent away the disciples, only to have to rejoin them later by walking across the waters of a lake.

'It is, generally speaking, John who knows the time of year, the time of day, where people sat, and how they got from one place to another' (Sayers 1943 p.33f). Naturally so, because the historical novelist supplies such details from imagination, to round out his story. It is, therefore, naive to suggest today that the filling in with plausible detail of gaps in the Synoptic account of the Passion shows this gospel's historical value, rather than its literary merit.

Any novelist, however, likes a few genuine background facts; and some details in John, such as the arcaded Pool of Bethesda, are confirmed by archaeology. Since

Jerusalem had been largely destroyed in 70 AD, its temple and priesthood gone forever, such details were probably culled from the memories of those of an earlier generation who had visited the city while its often magnificent architecture was still intact.

Fictitious Sources

Possibly my least popular contention will be that the 'Beloved Disciple', so much beloved by many scholars, is an invention; yet, if we consider him as a character in such a novel, that is his proper role, the fictitious witness. Historical novelists should offer plausible sources; and John is the only gospel which sees a need to authenticate its message in this way. (Luke mentions other writers and witnesses, but without claiming them as his sources, although clearly he did use some.) In ancient fiction, however, pseudo-authentication, explaining how the story came to be known from a 'reliable source', was standard practice.[16] So, in John, the writer asserts that the unnamed disciple, who with Peter followed the arrested Jesus, was known to the high priest, thus pre-empting the question as to how anything could have been learned by Jesus' followers about interrogations before Annas or Caiaphas. While this does not really explain how the writer comes also to be able to quote verbatim from Pilate's questioning of Jesus indoors (18.33-37, 19.8-11), it is a typical novelist's device, hinting at a not too clearly defined source of information, in order that the reader shall suspend disbelief at least until after finishing the tale.

John also uses the well-known ploy of having corroborative testimony to the identity of his fictious source. Consider first a modern example from *The Last of the Wine*, by Mary Renault, whose core theme is Socrates and his teaching, related by a fictional follower, Alexias. Her final chapter is rounded off with an appended note, subscribed by another Alexias, an officer in the Athenian cavalry under Alexander the Great. This note states that the officer had found the book amongst his late father's papers and realised that it must have been the work of his grandfather, the earlier Alexias; who had dropped dead whilst hunting, when aged about fifty-five. The writer has, he says, bound up the book, finished or not.

Renault has thus explained how the story might have survived in written form, while adding an extra layer of verisimilitude by attesting her fictional eyewitness by the hand of his fictional grandson. The aim is not deception; but the author owes it to her readers not to lessen their enjoyment by offering them a tale which plainly never could have become known. Of this ancient novelists were well aware. Indeed, the author of *Daphnis and Chloe* also uses a double technique, explaining in his prologue how in the Nymphs' wood he found the lovers' story told in a picture, and finishing the story with his finally united lovers decorating the cave of the Nymphs to honour their guardian deities.

The evangelist's aim is the same, his method more subtle but more emphatic. He introduces, as one of Jesus' first two recruits, an unnamed disciple, friend but not brother of Andrew (John 1.40f). He develops the still nameless disciple into Jesus' favourite disciple at the last supper, and at the crucifixion; in between, this disciple has followed the arrest party, with Peter, and entered the high priest's house. At the end of the crucifixion the evangelist states that '**This is vouched for by an eyewitness, whose evidence is to be trusted. He knows that he speaks the truth, so that you too may believe...**'(19.35): again, the extra layer of attestation; the witness is still not identified as the unnamed favourite, but the reader will probably take it so.

Closing the story.

John's final chapter ties up these and other loose ends. It is written in the form of an afterthought or appendix to a book which he had apparently concluded originally at 20.31, where Thomas's resounding statement of belief is followed by the ringing declaration that '**Many indeed and other were the signs which Jesus did in the presence of his disciples, which are not recorded in this book. These however have been written down so that you may believe that Jesus is the Messiah, the Son of God, and believing thus may have life in his name.**' Scholars have therefore mostly taken Chapter Twenty-One not as a genuine postscript by the author but as evidence of a second author, or at the least of a second edition. Seen as a novel, however, the book would not be complete without its epilogue, and at what point in his writing this inspiration visited the author is not important.

Here, after a hint to the reader by means of the only mention in the entire gospel of the sons of Zebedee, the writer lets Jesus imply, without actually saying so, that the anonymous disciple might live a very long time, and finally identifies his witness as the beloved disciple, the one who shared a couch with Jesus at the last supper. '**This is the disciple who has testified to these things**

and has written them down, and we know that his witness is true.'[17] Thus the reader has been encouraged to identify the favourite disciple with John bar Zebedee, and both of these with the notoriously long-lived disciple John of Ephesus, an eyewitness who might plausibly have been consulted by someone else who lived on to write in the second century.[18] It is good technique, when putting over such a dubious connection, to do it by leaving your readers to draw the conclusion for themselves, so that they may be too pleased by their own astuteness to question the evidence; as indeed they were, with the church soon taking this identification as fact. But apart from that, the scene by the lake forms a memorable epilogue.

Here, without the drama and tears of Easter morning, without Thomas's defiant scepticism, there is an idyllic scene; during which, nonetheless, Peter is challenged to the point of exasperation. As so often, translators have tended to smooth over any unbecoming emotion. What angers Peter is a continual scaling down of Jesus' expectations. First it is **'Simon, son of Jonah, do you love me better than anyone else does?'** and Peter, now, cannot repeat that boast. **'Yes, master,'** he says humbly, **'you know that I care about you'**. The second time the question is simply **'Do you love me?'** and Peter will not claim even as much as that. But the third time Jesus downshifts to challenge even Peter's minimal claim: '**Simon, son of Jonah, *do* you care about me?**' '**And Peter was vexed because on the third occasion what he asked was "Do you care about me?" and he said to him, "Master, you know everything, you know I care about you!"**' Then finally he is reinstated as leader of the apostles: **'Feed my flock'**.

'The ending of a novel needs to be tackled with great care, and a fault to be avoided is that of rushing it. Take time to let the reader off the hook, so that he doesn't feel hurried, and make sure that at least all the important ends of your plot are neatly tied off.' (Legat, 1993, p.74). In the passage cited earlier, Mary Renault did not merely accredit her 'eyewitness' but also assured us that he had gone on to live a relatively long life, blessed with children and grandchildren, before a quick and easy death; and that his grandson is sufficiently well off to be a cavalry officer, in a victorious army. Since the story had seen Alexias' family lose its wealth, and his city lose its wars, with the final chapter foreshadowing the unjust death of Socrates himself, such assurances are grateful to the reader. Our evangelist, too, at greater length, has tied up all loose ends to finish on a very positive note.

Signs and Wonders.

He has, however, left other difficulties in his book. No concern for plausibility was ever allowed to inhibit this author's taste for the impossible miracle. Quite deliberately, it seems, all his 'signs', whether culled from the Synoptics or entirely his own, have been heightened in order to leave no loophole for any explanation except Act of God.

As novelist he can devise, in his Galilean ministry, the Wedding at Cana; where the servants fill six twenty-gallon water-jars to the brim with water and promptly draw from them a superlative wine. Any faint possibility that water, stored overnight in vessels previously used for wine, might pass undetected by tipsy guests, has been carefully eliminated. Indeed, the specification of these jars as containing water according to the washing-customs of the Jews (John 2.6) implies that they would never have been used for anything but water.

Next, when healing a sick person unseen and at a distance (a case no doubt based on the Centurion's Slave, in Matthew and Luke, or the Syro-Phoenician Woman's Daughter in Mark) Jesus is not, in this gospel, even in the same town: from Cana he heals a boy lying sick at Capernaum.

The Feeding of the Five Thousand is already, as told by the Synoptics, an inexplicable miracle, needing only improvement in detail: Jesus now becomes the sole distributor, the twelve full baskets of fragments have *all* come from the five loaves, and the miraculous nature of the event is underlined by the crowd's response, hailing Jesus as the prophet and wanting to make him a king (John 6.14f.). Walking on the Water was perhaps one miracle from the earlier gospels which this writer found sufficiently marvellous: nonetheless, he makes clear that Jesus has walked three or four *miles* on the water, almost the full width of the lake (John 6.19, 21), thus ruling out any suggestion of wading out on a sandbank; and he underlines this with the bafflement of the crowd, who search where they last saw him, but only find him eventually back on the other shore.

Healings too are moved up into the category of the absolutely unheard of. Non-medical healings are sufficiently attested in the modern world to show that, whatever their *cause* or *explanation*, their *possibility* in the ancient world need not be doubted; but this is not to say that such healings, basically psychological, can flout the laws of nature, and in Mark they do not. In John, however, the cripple has been paralysed for thirty-eight years, unlike the youngster in the original story (Mark 2.5); the blind man has been blind from birth; and the dead man dead for four days in a hot climate. The scene when Jesus stands at the door of the tomb and calls the dead man forth is memorable, but, considered dispassionately, hardly credible.

Finally, when the supernatural quality of Jesus' risen body has been demonstrated by its appearance through locked doors (20.19, 26), its physical reality is tested by Thomas's unbelief. Whether we are to understand that he actually puts his finger in the marks of the nails and his hand into the spear-wound (both spear and nails having been added to the tradition by this author), or does not, no doubt is left that he could have done so. Even in the epilogue, the moving scene of reconciliation by the lakeside has to be prefaced by Jesus not only guiding the fishers to a clearly miraculous and obscurely symbolic catch of 153 fish,[19] but having a fire ready for them when they bring their catch ashore (21.9-13). No leeway is to be left for mere visions of a spirit without physical substance.

Alarms and excursions

Nothing could more surely mark John's 'gospel' as an ancient novel than its plethora of dangers and escapes. Certainly Mark claims that early in the Galilean ministry some Pharisees and Herodians consulted as to how to destroy Jesus, and Luke suggests that Jesus had to beware of Herod, but nothing serious ever follows. John, having signalled early the ideas of distrust and secrecy (2.24, 3.12), proceeds to the Judaeans wanting to kill Jesus (5.16-18), a recurring motif thereafter, with Jesus twice escaping stoning, twice escaping arrest, twice leaving Judaea for safety and three times returning by stealth. At the Last Supper we have the covert signalling of the traitor's identity to the beloved disciple; and even after the crucifixion the disciples must still secure the doors 'for fear of the Judaeans'. This is the very stuff of the ancient 'romance'.

A creative approach

Even conservative or moderate opinion has long had some doubts as to how far the evangelist is to be relied upon. **'The Fourth Evangelist does not reproduce the tradition as a chronicler would represent it... It is quite out of place to test these stories by the kind of historical standard we apply to the Markan and the Lukan stories'**, said Vincent Taylor (1949: p.165). **'Throughout his gospel [John] seems to handle his historical material with considerable freedom in the interests of theological truth'**, suggested R.H. Lightfoot (1950: p.77).

Such reservations, however, fall well short of the claim made here, that the author of John is a novelist, writing fiction in the style of his time. Even Culpepper's *Anatomy of the Fourth Gospel*, wholly given to the analysis of John as a work of literature, avoids describing the gospel outright as unhistorical; while Lindars, Moody and Stibbe have continued to uphold an authentic independent tradition behind some parts of this gospel.

Stibbe, citing Dodd, Robinson and Hengel in his support, claims that there is now **'an intellectually rigorous case'** made out for John's historical value. With all respect for the integrity and scholarship of those concerned, however, this is to try to have one's cake and eat it. Stibbe, for example, emphasizes the creativity of the author, but only allows him to have invented such details as it is scarcely possible to uphold as fact. For example, in his study of John 18 and 19 (1992, pp.171f, 192), Stibbe concedes that details of the arrest scene are **'redescribed by the story-teller with narrative licence', 'an obvious example of dramatic hyperbole',** and **'hardly an historical reminiscence'**; but the only further concession he makes (mistakenly, as we shall see) against John's historical veracity concerns the date of the crucifixion.

To stress the historical reliability of John is seriously to underestimate the desire of creative authors to fashion wholly new scenes of their own. Such scenes are the author's ambition and delight, as near as any human comes to creation *ex nihilo*, immensely satisfying when done. Once it is admitted that the Fourth Evangelist was a truly creative author, one must expect him to have created new scenes, from no source whatever, simply to meet the needs of his story (e.g. John 7.1-9; 21.15-23) or to express his theology (e.g. John 4.1-42; 6.22-71). It follows that, while it is possible that he *might* have used some otherwise unknown tradition as a basis for such an episode, it is both risky and unnecessary to assume that he did.

It seems sounder to suppose, therefore, that, given its highly creative author, not one single word in John can be taken as fact on that gospel's sole authority. Nothing in John should be accepted as historical unless, and no farther than, it is also known from more reliable sources; nor can anything in John be used to corroborate the Synoptics, from whom, if it agrees with them, it has probably been taken.[20] This 'gospel' is a historical novel, a mixture of fact and fiction in which the fictional, it will be shown, hugely predominates; a work written, not to deceive (for its readers would already have been instructed in the basic facts) but as a new interpretation to reveal the full significance of Jesus. As history, John is always very doubtful; as fiction, it is often inspired.

2

Problems with the Text

Even in our topmost layer, however, which is John's gospel
as it is now, traces of some earlier version are apparent.
There is, in fact, a general agreement amongst scholars
that there was an earlier document, copied or adapted or
rewritten once or several times to create the gospel we have
now; by one man or by two; or by a 'Johannine school'
of admiring disciples (Hengel 1989, pp.74-102). There is
considerable agreement about the most basic evidence, in
the form of puzzles and discrepancies indicating changes
to an original text; but none as to the nature or form of
the original document. So, after the basic evidence has
been considered, it may be worth putting forward a new
suggestion.

Not a Seamless Whole

The gospel's penultimate verse, could it be taken at face
value, would be enough to show that this is not completely
the work of a single eye-witness; for '**We know that his
witness is true**' (John 21.24), plainly means that 'we',
who are responsible for publication, are people other than
the witness whom we trust. Since, however, it has already
been argued that John is fiction, such a statement could
well be the work of a skilful novelist. Yet the narrative

version of John which we now possess presents abundant problems pointing to a much more complex process of composition than the mere writing of a novel or the careful edition of an earlier text.

There are many odd features in the actual writing: peculiar joins, jumps in time, inconsistencies in the story, illogicalities of time and place and odd breaks in the theme; all which, if puzzling as anomalies in the work of a talented novelist, would be still more so in that of a conscientious biographer or a later editor. These perplexing problems, commonly styled *aporias* (puzzles), are all the more odd because they appear in the work of an author who can write as fluent and coherent a story as, for example, that of the Samaritan Woman (4.1-42).

A Confusion of Aporias

The *aporias* strongly suggest that changes have been made at some time to an original text, or texts. A very clear example is John 14.31b, where Jesus says, '**Get up, let us be going from here**', yet nobody moves for three whole chapters, until Jesus finally (18.1) leaves the house with his disciples.

R.T. Fortna (1970, pp.2-12) says that scholars have noted '**many inconsistencies, disjunctures and hard connections, even contradictions**'; and it is such contextual confusions which he rightly holds to be the least subjective evidence available for the way in which the gospel came to be composed. These *'aporias'* show, he suggests, that the gospel has been reworked, '**the seams** [where the text appears to have been 'cobbled together']

being due for the most part to the transition not from oral to literary form, but *from one literary form to another*' (my italics). Such a transition, from one literary form to another, is precisely what will be suggested here; but the two types of literature are not those suggested by Fortna.

Nonetheless, it is also strongly held by some that the whole book shows the style and thought of a single author (Barrett 1978, pp.5-26; Lindars 1971, pp.15-42). The most obvious presumption from the textual evidence must then be that the author himself rewrote or expanded an earlier work of his own; as Hanson (1991, p.18) and Lindars agree, although both assign Chapter 21 to a later hand and allow occasional verses to be editorial comment.

That John is one writer's work is perhaps corroborated to some degree by the errors which remain, since mistakes in one's own work are the hardest to notice. Rewriting by the author, and not by a later redactor, would best account for the residue of error; otherwise it could only be true that **'the final editor was a person of extraordinary carelessness or lack of perception, for he has left *aporias* in great abundance throughout his work'** (Hanson 1991, p.8).

Jumps in Time

There are, for example, abrupt shifts in the narrative: **'So they picked up stones to hurl at him. Jesus however hid himself and left the temple. *And as he was walking along* (*paragōn*), he saw a man blind from birth...'** (John 8.59, 9.1). The second verse follows the first so oddly, switching without pause or explanation from a moment of concealed flight to strolling openly through the streets of Jerusalem with the disciples, that it is no wonder that these verses have now been divided by the arbitrary insertion of a chapter-ending.

The miracle at Cana is rounded off with the comment, **'This, the first of his signs, Jesus performed at Cana in Galilee, and displayed his glory; and his disciples believed in him'**; followed by the remark that **'After this he went down to Capernaum with his mother and his brothers and his disciples, and they stayed there a few days.'**[21] Then, with no concern for probability, the author announces that it is nearly Passover, and sends Jesus straight back to Jerusalem, which he had only left the week before (John 2.1-13).

Whenever the novelist wants Jesus in Jerusalem, he simply puts him there (3.13; 5.1); equally abruptly, **'after this'** he moves Jesus *from* Jerusalem to **'the other side of the sea of Galilee'** (6.1) since he now requires a Galilean setting. If he wishes the same crowd who were miraculously fed on the east shore to be back on the west side next day, in order to hear Jesus (who has made his own miraculous crossing of the lake during the night) declaim that he is the Bread of Life, then, by a very convenient coincidence, fishing-boats from Tiberias turn up on cue and ferry the crowd across (6.23f).

Geographical Puzzles

Here and there the geography lacks logic. If the disciples had been, as John 4.1 asserts, baptising on a grand scale, they could hardly have done so anywhere but in the Jordan;

certainly not in or around Jerusalem, in the Kidron brook or the pool of Siloam. Yet, while the shortest route, much used by pilgrims, to Galilee from Jerusalem was indeed through Samaria (a fact known to anyone who had read Josephus),[22] the Jordan valley itself offered the shorter road for anyone already down in its valley. Why then is it necessary for Jesus to go through Samaria (4.4)?

The abruptness of Jesus' move to Galilee (6.1) was noted above; its geography is also suspect, since either Jesus goes directly from Jerusalem to an uninhabited spot on the farther, foreign, side of the lake, *trailed by this same crowd all the way from Jerusalem*; or, although the wording implies that he *should* be setting out from Jerusalem, he has already been in Galilee long enough to do further healings and attract a *Galilean* crowd, which somehow follows him round to the far side of the lake. (Jesus himself has, presumably, crossed with the disciples in the boat in which they make their return journey.) It seems likely that this results simply from the careless interweaving of two different documents, since the author can, when he tries, write clear and coherent narrative.

Two Ways with Time

Such problems with times and places suggest that the author has two modes, in only one of which are consecutive incidents linked together. Thus from 1.19 to 2.12 the indications are continuous: **'at Bethany'; 'on the next day'; 'the next day again'; 'the next day (...) he decided to go to Galilee'; 'On the third day there was a wedding at Cana '; 'After this he went down to Capernaum (...) for a few days'**. The time-scheme may sound breathless, but passes well enough in reading. But then 2.13 abruptly announces that the Passover was near and Jesus went to Jerusalem.

To take this as following from 2.12 is, as stated above, to make Jesus return to the city little more than a week after he had left it. 2.13, then, is making no attempt to fit into a detailed or plausible schedule, but aims merely to introduce a dramatic scene without delay. In this second mode each episode closes on a good line, here the astonished and outraged **'This temple has taken forty-six years to build,**[23] **and you are going to build it in three days?'** (2.20); and there is often comment from the author before the next scene. In this case, 2.21-5 briefly explains Jesus' saying, and his far-seeing unwillingness to trust to his adherents; then, (3.1f.) Nicodemus appears (presumably at this time and in Jerusalem, although that is not stated), and, after what Jesus says to him, again comes comment, this time a deeper, theological, statement. (The element of night time visiting was probably added later, to hint at the motif of secrecy and danger which is the essence of the Greek novel. John contains five evasions, two escapes from stoning, several secret journeys, and a coded signal to identify a traitor.)[24]

These two distinct modes alternate throughout the gospel, and it might be reasonable to suppose that the 'consecutive' passages were intended from the first to be part of the novelistic narrative which we now have, while scenes begun or ended abruptly come from a document of a different kind. However, some such scenes have been greatly expanded, so that their structure is not now so clear. For example, we have seen above that at the Last Supper the most obvious of closing lines, **'Get up, let**

us be going from here' (John 14.31b) now appears in mid-discourse, and nobody moves for another eighty-six verses. The expansion of an original draft which this suggests would also explain a second noted *aporia*: Jesus says (16.5), **'Now I am going to the one who sent me, and none of you asks me "Where are you going?"'**, which is not consistent with Thomas's previous grumble, **'Lord, we don't know where you are going. How can we know the way?'** (14.5), still less with Peter's yet earlier, direct **'Lord, where are you going?'** (13.36). Such expansions and interpolations seem clear evidence for the rewriting and expansion of a first written document in one style into a second in another.

Interpolations

A glaring example of the interpolation of one story into another is found in John Ch.7. Here 7.14 seems a typical 'abrupt' opening: **'*About the middle of the feast* Jesus went into the temple and taught'**; 7.37 is similar but specifies a later day: **'*On the last day, the great day of the feast*, Jesus stood up and proclaimed...'** Two short scenes, then, allocated to different days; but during the first one, in the middle of the feast, the chief priests and Pharisees send Levites (in this context, temple police) to arrest Jesus (7.32); no more is heard of them until they report failure on the last day of the feast *two or three days later* (7.45f.); yet the entire episode is set within the temple precinct, where both Jesus and the Levites were.

This odd time-scheme is not, like some previous examples, merely apparent, resulting from the use of two modes in the narration; nor is it credible. It can only have been created through the slightly careless expansion of an original episode by the insertion of the short Come to Me and Drink speech (7.37-44); and it seems most likely that the insertion, which is complete in itself, had already been written.[25]

There is another obvious interpolation where not action but a speech has been interrupted. John 7.19-24, dealing with Moses and the Sabbath, would fit perfectly onto the end of John 5, where Jesus has just introduced Moses into an argument about the keeping of the Sabbath, ending: **'But if you do not believe his** (Moses') **writings, how will you believe my words?'** (5.47). After the whole of Chapter Six, and then (John 7.1-18) Jesus' deception of his brothers and some verses in which he is criticised as uneducated, the discourse abruptly switches back to Moses: **'Did not Moses give you the law? Yet none of you keeps the law. Why do you seek to kill me?'.** It appears that, into what was probably first written as a single speech, the author has inserted a lengthy Galilean section (6.1-7.9); then, having manoeuvred Jesus back in the temple again, the author allows him the rest of his 'Moses' speech.

This accords perfectly with the suggested pattern of new material being grafted into an original script. (It is close to Lindars' view that the author put together sundry traditional stories and sayings and ingrafted his own homilies; provided that we take it that both elements were written down before the grafting.) The **'I am the bread of life'** speech, however (6.35-58), seems to be a further insertion, this time in the Galilean section. For Jesus at Capernaum is no longer, we find, talking to the common people who have trailed him to and fro across the lake, but to the Judaeans (6.52), in a speech reminiscent of the Jerusalem **'I am the light of the world'** (12.44-50) and **'I am the good shepherd'** (10.7-18) speeches, and in vigorous controversy like that of Chapters 5 and 8. If most of this speech had originally been drafted for a Jerusalem context, and then moved, complete with Judaeans, up to Galilee,[26] and re-sited in Capernaum as a sequel to the Feeding of the Crowd, that would explain how the Judaeans suddenly appear in Galilee to take over the debate, making little sense of the claim that Jesus now stays in Galilee to avoid them (John 7.1).

Another sign of the insertion of material may be found in the numbering of two miracles as the first (2.11) of Jesus' signs, and as *the second done in Galilee* (4.54);[27] which seems pointless, since no numbering is given to the equally impressive Galilean miracles in Chapter 6. A possible explanation would be that these two Galilean miracles, Turning Water into Wine, and Healing the Nobleman's Son, which are not borrowings from Mark but devised by our author, were first composed as a single piece, 2.1-12 with 4.46b-54; with the second miracle perhaps set in Capernaum (like the Healing of the Centurion's Slave in Matthew and Luke, from which the idea of healing without seeing the patient was probably taken); Jesus is said to have gone to Capernaum after the first miracle at Cana (John 2.12). Later, the Jerusalem scenes with the Cleansing of the Temple and with Nicodemus, the second reference to the Baptist, and the newly invented story of the Samaritan woman, would all have been inserted into the earlier version; and the second miracle might then have been made more striking by putting the healer at Cana again, miles away from the sick boy (4.46a).

The First Document

Yet if there is general consensus that there are a great many oddities in the text, and some agreement that the best explanation of these would be (following Fortna) the author's combination of what had been written in two different modes, there is still none about the form and nature of the original first document. Morton Smith and Wills each hypothesise a lost gospel used by both John and Mark; a 'Miracles Gospel' or Fortna's 'Signs Gospel' are also surmised; other scholars, including Lindars and Hengels, propound different schemes for the rewriting or editing of the author's first script, by himself or by one or by several others. Here it will be suggested that the first version was in the form of a draft for a Greek tragedy about Jesus; the author having intended a play but then, for some reason which can only be surmised, decided to turn it into a novel. Such a rewriting from play to novel could, we shall see, account for each and every discrepancy and oddity in the text.

3

Greek Theatre

Next, for the general reader, a brief introduction to the classical Greek theatre, to give a context against which to judge the arguments and visualise the examples which will be put forward. The relevance of Greek drama to this twenty-first century, when the study of the classics no longer plays a significant part in secondary education, lies in the depth and strength of the problems and dilemmas of such characters as Oedipus, Antigone, Orestes, Electra and Iphigenia, persons from legend who were brought to tragic life on the Athenian stage. The human condition was explored as never before, not through literature but on the stage; the audience not only heard the great affirmations and deep emotions expressed in words, but saw the characters play out their fates, for good or ill, before their watching eyes.

Greek Drama in the First Century AD

Even so, it might be asked how relevant could the great Greek tragedies, the works of Aeschylus, Sophocles, and Euripides, all of whom wrote in the fifth century BC, have been to the author of a Christian gospel in, say, 95-105 AD? Those great Athenian playwrights were dead half a century before the birth of Alexander the Great in 356

AD: five centuries of conquest and war, political upheaval and major cultural change had passed before this gospel was written in or near the reign of the Roman emperor Trajan (98-117 AD).

However, the enduring legacy of Alexander's empire was the Greek language, spread, across all the Near East, together with some degree of Greek culture. The well educated could speak and write Greek correctly and fluently, as does our fourth evangelist. There was also a rough, *'koinē' or* 'common' Greek, so widely used as a second language that it seems likely that in Palestine Jesus and his disciples would also have spoken it. Amongst Latin speakers, too, the better educated were taught classical Greek. Everywhere the great Greek dramas were commonly used as school-texts. And when the aggressively pagan Julian (emperor, 361-3 AD) forbade to Christians this customary use of classical texts in schools, a Christian scholar, Apollinaris the Syrian, promptly composed as substitutes a Homeric epic, Platonic dialogues, comedies in the style of Menander and tragedies in that of Euripides, all on biblical themes.[28]

Early in the first century, so in Jesus' lifetime, there was a theatre in Jerusalem; possibly also one at Sepphoris, a new town only a few miles from Nazareth, although that one was more probably built a little later. Certainly Jesus seems to have used the Greek word *hypokritēs*, play-actor, to condemn insincerity.[29] New Greek plays were still written (including some by Jews, on biblical themes) and contests held to reward the best new plays; and the texts of some classical plays suggest that they have been cut and altered by producers eager to introduce extra spectacle.[30] In western Turkey, the Roman province called

Asia, where, traditionally, the gospel of John originated, the 'Ionian' Greek cities, Pergamum, Smyrna, Ephesus and many others,[31] all had their theatres. Inscriptions tell of drama festivals still held at Ancyra in 128 AD and at Aphrodisias in 180 AD;[32] while in Athens the great festival of Dionysus was still celebrated with competing tragedies in 96 AD. Any well educated Christian, and particularly one from Asia, would certainly have been familiar with some of the great Greek plays from school, may also have read them for pleasure, and even occasionally seen them performed. So our author would have known the fifth century plays, but probably imagined them as performed in a later type of theatre.

Staging of a Greek Tragedy.

To the Greeks, a 'tragedy' meant only a serious play, and some have happy outcomes; but all centre on the troubles and suffering of the central character. I shall suggest that that elusive first version of John, for which so many hypotheses have been advanced, was a draft for just such a Greek tragedy; a draft which the author later rewrote, with much additional material, to turn it instead into a historical novel of the kind then in fashion.

Like all drama, Greek plays were essentially, not words on paper, but words declaimed or sung, and actions performed, before the spectators in a theatre (*theatron*, a place where *hoi theomenoi*, the watchers, could watch [*theaomai*] a performance). The plays should therefore be imagined in production.

The actual setting for which these Greek plays had been written and in which they were performed had, by the first century AD, changed greatly in appearance from the earliest theatres, but little in essentials. The very first, the theatre of Dionysus at Athens and the place from which all Greek theatre sprang, had been erected early in the fifth century, reshaped by Pericles midway through that century, and rebuilt under Lycurgus in the fourth century; but probably showed from the beginning what were certainly the key features of any later theatre.[33]

Drama seems to have developed from the dithyrambs sung and danced at the feasts of Dionysus by a *choros* (hereafter chorus), and remained simply one part of the very large and important part played by music, singing and dancing in the religious, civic and communal life of Athens (Wilson 2000, pp.11-24). So Greek drama was always a musical performance; we may think of it as developing from choral song and dance, through oratorio to something between opera and a Hollywood musical, but invariably with a dancing, singing chorus.

Thespis was perhaps the first bard who transformed himself from soloist into actor; Aeschylus later added a second actor, and Sophocles is supposed to have added the third. The chorus remained dramatically important in the fifth century, participating in the action or commenting on it, or dancing as they sang, emphasizing with mime what was happening. (Think of the chorus of smugglers in Carmen, doing a rhythmic four-step to mime 'toiling up a mountainside'.[34]) So the first essential for a Greek theatre was an *orchēstra* (hereafter orchestra), a flat, often circular, open space where choruses sang and danced. Not until many centuries later was the name applied to the place in a theatre where musicians were grouped, and then to the musicians themselves; here, the only musician was an *aulos* (double pipe) player, standing probably beside the central altar. The chorus would usually enter the orchestra by one of the two *eisodoi* (entrances), also called *parodoi* (passages), which ran, on either side, between the stage-wall structure (*skēnē*) and the tiers of seating.

The *skēnē* (hereafter 'skene') was a wall, with a large double-door at its centre. On top of the skene ran a walkway – perhaps a secondary development -- called the *theologeion*, the 'place from which the gods spoke', as many plays require them to do. Mortals might appear there too, but in that case the walkway simply represented a towering cliff or the roof of a palace. Access would have been by some ladder behind the skene, probably an open stair of flat steps; for a deity must be able to make a dignified entry, while an actor playing a human scrambling onto a roof, or scaling a cliff, can easily simulate difficulty.

The stage seems to have originated as no more than the two or three steps up to the broader plinth appropriate in Greek architecture for a really important building; whose facade the skene basically resembled and often represented in the play (see *Appendix A*). The actors entered either by the *eisodoi* or through the central doorway in the skene. Although some scholars argue that no such stage existed in the earliest theatre,[35] that has no great relevance here, since, long before the first century AD, stages of stone had certainly been introduced, and then made higher, rising perhaps as much as ten foot above the ground; the skene itself, also of stone now and certainly with a central doorway, had developed an upper storey; and gods might appear aloft suspended by a crane, the *mechanē*. Thus we can be sure that, by the first century AD, a would-be playwright could take for granted the three basics of a (circular) orchestra; a skene with central doorway and a practicable higher level; and a high stage whose access from the level of the orchestra was, judging by the Hellenistic example which survives at Epidaurus, by ramps at either end.

A widely used piece of apparatus was a movable platform, the *ekkuklēma* (hereafter 'ekkyklema'), which could be wheeled out, through the central doorway, onto the stage; particularly to present an interior scene. For example, Aristophanes (*Acharnians* (ll.91-2) has 'Euripides' wheeled out on it when '**at work upstairs**'; and later there is a Roman mosaic showing it in use,[36] with three comic actors seated round a small table on a low platform with three steps at its front end. Such steps would allow the actors to descend easily to the main stage when the action moved from that 'interior' setting. Aristophanes' *Clouds*, for example, opens with Strepsiades and his son in their beds; once they have risen and 'gone out' down the steps of the ekkyklema, this can be withdrawn and the beds removed.

Setting the Scene

I find the key to understanding Greek theatrical production in Aristotle's *Poetics*, a short work dealing mainly with the art of the playwright. As soon as Aristotle has introduced the subject of drama, he pronounces the dictum: '**Imitation** (*mimēsis*, from which English 'mime' and 'mimicry') **is a natural human activity, from**

childhood onwards' (*Poetics, 4.2*). Precisely; and the conventions of Greek drama are those of children at play. The actors and the chorus must, by word and action, tell the audience where they are, and induce their hearers to use their own imagination to see more than they are shown. (So it was too in the Shakespearean theatre, which frankly called its actors 'players': '**Think, when we speak of horses, you do see them…**')

The misconception that every feature which is mentioned must be realistically represented led, in the last century, to some very far-fetched suggestions for staging particular plays. Certainly imagination was often helped along by using simple props, and by appropriate actions; but description in more detail tells the audience how to interpret what they are seeing, just as a child, setting foot on a bottom step, will tell a playmate, 'And now I'm starting to climb the mountain.' So, when Strepsiades says '**Do you see that little door and that little house?**' (Aristophanes, *The Clouds*, l.92), he is telling the audience how they are, in this instance, to regard the sizable central doorway; and this will probably be reinforced by a stooping attitude adopted by the actors when they use the door to enter the 'Thinkery' of Socrates. Rehm explains this usage well when he explains that in *Ion* the chorus of Athenian women, newly arrived to see the sights of Delphi '**create the sights primarily out of their words and gestures, and the spectators follow the verbal cues to project the (***imaginary***) sculptured images onto the conventional skene façade**' (Rehm 1994, p.135f). A statue or two might, I suggest, be set against the skene-wall, but the words and gestures multiply these, through the spectator's imagination, into the many monuments of Delphi.

As a further example, Evadne, in Euripides' *Suppliant Women*, leaps from a cliff, onto her husband's funeral pyre, so as to join him in death. Naturally she must, like Tosca, fall safely to somewhere out of sight. Presumably she jumps from the walkway on the top of the skene wall; but her climb to the top, and the fact that she must, theoretically, fall onto the pyre of her husband Capaneus, have caused great difficulty. The chorus ask **'Why does she, climbing that path, stand on the lofty crag which overhangs the temple?'**, and it has been supposed that she must therefore be in their view and genuinely climbing; Rehm (1994, p.130) even suggests that she might climb **'part of the theatre cavea** (*tiers of seating*) **itself, up the supporting wall alongside of the eisodos'**. But this is unnecessary: more practically, the chorus *tell* us where Evadne is, and what they see her doing, before she, climbing the last steps of a ladder behind the skene, [37] comes slowly into view, visibly toiling upwards, one step at a time, until finally she steps out onto the theologeion itself. She 'plays' the action of climbing, the chorus add verisimilitude with their verbal description. Nor need she later be shown, lifeless on her husband's tomb, as Webster (1970, p.159) envisaged: Evadne has told us where she will fall, we see her jump and disappear behind the skene, and that suffices.

Similarly, the central doorway represents whatever it is said to be. It can as easily be the tomb of Darius, from which his spirit is called forth, as the entrance to Agammemnon's palace, the door to Socrates' humble dwelling, or the city gates of Thebes.[38]

A good example of this style of playing can be found at the opening of Sophocles' *Philoctētēs*. Odysseus as he enters ostensibly tells his companion, but really informs the audience, that '**this is the beach of the sea-girt soil of Lemnos, untrodden, uninhabited by man**'. He has entered therefore through the parodos, at the level of the orchestra (where there is as yet no chorus present to hide him from view) and he sends young Neoptolemos ahead to seek the cave where Philoctētēs lives, a '**two-mouthed rock so shaped by nature as in winter to provide a seat in the sun twice over, while in summer the breeze blowing through the cave from one entry to the other induces sleep**'. The repeated emphasis on the double entrance has told the audience that the central doorway, with its double-door set wide, is now Philoctētēs' cave, which will be the focus of the entire play. This Neoptolemus then espies, and calls his news back to Odysseus, who asks '**Up above, or down below? I don't perceive it.**' '**Right up here** (*tod' exuperthe*)' says the young man, pointing, as he 'climbs' the steps, and then calls 'down' his report that it is empty but obviously inhabited.[39]

Costumes, Masks and Props

Yet, if true realism was not needed, communication with the audience was essential. Costume had to be appropriate to the character: a rich robe for a king, plainer robes for his councillors, ankle length dresses for the maidens, shorter dresses and shorter hair for their attendants. The masks for the actors existed not merely so that each actor could appear in two or three roles in the same play (no more than three actors being allowed), but also, by the clearly drawn expressions on their larger than life-size faces, and their appropriate hair styles, to show even to more distant spectators the age, sex, and perhaps the dominant mood of the character being played. Then, if, for example, Clytemnestra's honeyed words issued from a mask suggesting anger or hate, the audience could see for themselves that her character was deceitful. The choruses also were sometimes, and perhaps always, masked – other considerations apart, probably a necessity when male singers were appearing as women.

Simple props were used: a chair for a king to sit in judgement, spears and helmets for his guards, a bier for a dying queen, and so forth. Assisted by these visual aids, and a simple mode of production in an unelaborate setting, the audiences were treated to great drama in splendid verse, or to hilarious, and very bawdy, comedy.

EXCURSUS Uses of the Ekkyklema

Structure and Design

It may help to envisage Greek drama more clearly if we consider briefly some possible uses of that ever present prop, the ekkyklema. In Appendix A I argue that, contrary to the theories of some leading modern scholars, both the skene with its central doorway and the ekkyklema existed in the very earliest purpose-built theatre, although neither was then *used* in all the ways which developed later and need not, therefore, have been yet of the size which later uses appear to require.

Particular instances of the ekkyklema's use can only ever be inferences from the texts, since these give no explicit stage directions. We do not know its design or dimensions; but I will suggest that the basic structure of the developed ekkyklema was a wooden platform, some two feet or thirty inches high, and, later at least, some eight feet wide by ten feet long; for it could hardly have been much smaller if it was to have room for several actors at a time, often with some item(s) of indoor furniture. It would have rolled out, as Aristophanes implies, on wheels (which would be best fitted out of the way, *inside* the platform) and guided by the sides of the doorway; but never rolled out to its full length, nor completely withdrawn. Its sides could come down close to the floor on which it stood, and the front and rear ends would each consist of three steps, so that actors could easily mount or leave it. The earliest ekkyklema, however, need only, for the uses which I shall suggest as its first purpose, have been, say, six feet wide, and might have had steps at its forward end only.

For the most basic use for the apparatus, when nothing more was required, would, I suggest, have been to be firmly bolted down with its front end protruding *under* the central doors of the skene, to make the extra steps proper to a palace or a temple. This would add appropriate dignity to the important building or city which the skene very often represents, and would allow an actor to make a more impressive entrance. (The doors would then simply have been made to fit *above* these steps; and would always have had the ekkyklema underneath them, in one position or another.)

Thus Agammemnon, in Aeschylus' play, would, from the orchestra, tread to his doom, on the crimson tapestries which his treacherous wife has had spread for him (*l.910*), up six or seven steps, not three or four; so making very visible an impressively ill-omened exit into his palace. Again, at the opening of Euripides' *Suppliant Women,* when Adrastus is seen lying '**in the doorway**', the extra height of the ekkyklema would let him be more easily seen by all.[40] The many vase paintings of scenes from plays are not necessarily accurate representations of their staging; but the fact that in them temples and palaces are almost always shown with two or three steps is a clear indication of what public taste expected, and what would therefore serve as a useful visual clue in setting the scene.

Aeschylus and the Ekkyklema

Possible further uses of the ekkyklema may be considered here in relation to all the surviving works of Aeschylus.[41] For *The Persians,* the ekkyklema could, throughout the play, protrude well forward, probably furnished with some altar or memorial to mark it as the tomb of Darius; and later, when forcefully invoked, his ghost would appear from the shadows, mount the rear steps and '**proceed onto the high crest of the barrow**' (*l.659*). For *Prometheus Bound* the ekkyklema would again have been prominently placed from the start of the play, enhanced with some sloping superstructure to heighten the 'rock' against which Prometheus will lie chained; a superstructure that might be fitted with sockets or staples so that the actor who plays Hephaestus could more easily chain and stake Prometheus convincingly. (See n.50 below for how a stake might have been hammered 'through' his body.) The skene, its architectural façade irrelevant, here represents the 'towering rocky crags' of the opening speech. In this case, however, at the end of the play, when Zeus does '**cleave the jagged cliff with thunder and the fiery thunderbolt**', the doors would be hauled open from inside, no doubt with suitable 'noises off', and Prometheus would be withdrawn, to suffer in '**the sunless realm of**

Hades and the gloomy deep by Tartarus'; with his loyal chorus of the Daughters of Ocean perhaps gallantly following the ekkyklema.

In *Suppliant Maidens* the ekkyklema would be, throughout the play, the rocky hill or outcrop '**belonging to the assembled gods**', near which Danaus tells his daughters to sit. On the platform might be statues whose emblems proclaimed them as Zeus, Apollo, Poseidon and Hermes, and a single altar. Grouped around the shrine, with some actually on the stage or at least on its steps, the maidens can sing their part, until later the friendly king of Argos tells them to '**come down to this level precinct**', and they descend reluctantly to the orchestra, protesting that it does not offer the safer sanctuary of consecrated ground. When Danaus from his 'vantage point' on the high ground sees the pursuer's ships arriving, the leader of the chorus presumably runs up to see for herself, since she comments on how fast they are coming; and when the Egyptian herald or captain appears, the chorus crowd back, seeking the protection of the gods, up onto the steps, closer to the shrine; and there they struggle desperately to remain, until rescue arrives in the nick of time.

Similarly, in *Seven against Thebes* I suggest that the ekkyklema should serve throughout, furnished with suitable statues, as the shrine of the 'ancestral deities' of Thebes, around which the chorus of maidens will cluster. (In line with Aeschylus' usage in *Suppliant Maidens* and *Prometheus Bound,* the central doorway is not here used at all for entry.) Again, as in *Suppliant Maidens*, the chorus are ordered, before Eteocles goes to muster his seven champions, to move away from the images (*l.265*), and so, presumably, down to the orchestra, where they can better perform the many verses they have to sing later, together or as separate groups with different viewpoints.

In the later trilogy of plays, *Agamemnon, The Offering Bearers* and *Eumenides,* Aeschylus is using a more developed stagecraft. The use of the ekkyklema to provide steps for the palace doorway in *Agamemnon* has already been suggested; but one almost certain example of the ekkyklema used to reveal an indoor scene comes later in the same play when, after death-cries from behind the skene, Clytemnestra is wheeled out standing over the bodies of her victims, Agamemnon and Cassandra;[42] Agamemnon, or perhaps an extra or a dummy, is still sprawled in his 'silver-sided' bath,[43] with a dummy Cassandra beside him,[44] both partly covered with one of those crimson tapestries, which has been used to entangle the king for slaughter. (The convention here is the reverse of the cinematic one by which our viewpoint can start outside a building and then zoom *in* to see what is inside; the ekkyklema brings the interior scene *out* to be seen.) When Clytemnestra has finished browbeating the chorus of citizens, the ekkyklema can be withdrawn, and Clytemnestra should follow it,[45] to re-enter later (*l.1654*) when fighting between the men of Argos and Aegisthus' retainers seems imminent.

In *The Offering Bearers,* the immediate sequel to *Agamemnon,* I suggest that the ekkyklema, adorned with some 'monument' or 'headstone', would represent the barrow appropriate for Agamemnon's grave, to which the offerings are brought in the opening scene. It would be withdrawn as the chorus leave in procession at the close of that act, thus assisting the imagined transition from the grave back to the palace.[46] Later, when Aegisthus has been killed off-stage, one way of presenting the following scene, without accepting Weir Smyth's premature display of dead Aegisthus,[47] would be to have the slave rush out to the top of the steps at the palace door, shouting the alarm (*l.875*) and pointing back inside as he calls Clytemnestra forth from the 'women's quarters'. She, too, comes out to the top of the steps and questions the slave; then the slave, when Clytemnestra calls for a battleaxe, makes himself scarce, and Orestes steps out, attended by Pylades, pointing back inside from the top of the steps' to '**that man who's had enough**' (the dead Aegisthus) and, after argument – I envisage Clytemnestra backing away down the steps, but being seized by the wrist to prevent escape -- takes his mother back inside. The chorus sing, and only then is Orestes rolled out on the ekkyklema, with the corpses of both Aegisthus and Clytemnestra at his feet, and the tapestry which was used in the murder of Agamemnon now displayed to prove his mother's guilt, thus dramatically mirroring Clytemnestra's display of bodies in the first play. The ekkyklema would be withdrawn at the end of the play, during the final chorus.

In *Eumenides*, the final play in the trilogy, I hold that the ekkyklema will not be required during opening of the play, other than as the steps to the temple doors. The Pythia, Apollo's prophetess at Delphi, enters from the side, introducing herself, and naming the central doorway as Apollo's shrine, by means of a long invocation to the gods of prophecy, delivered from the ekkyklema 'platform'. She enters the shrine, only to shriek with horror, collapse, and reappear on hands and knees, as Taplin insists; pushing one door partly open as she crawls out, easily visible because of the extra height the ekkylema gives her. Then, after her first five lines, she recovers enough to haul herself to her feet. As she describes the shocking scene within, the doors burst open as half the chorus of Erinyes, the Furies who pursue anyone who kills a blood-relation, burst out on the stage, giving the startled audience a moment of shuddering horror at their hideous appearance. They are followed by the ekkyklema on which Orestes is clinging to a replica of the Delphi 'navel-stone', with behind him an actor as Apollo;[48] and the other half of the chorus, who run in nimbly over its back steps, as the ekkyklema is rolled fully forward. Then the whole chorus collapse back into their exhausted sleep, thus completing in plain view the whole interior scene which so horrified the priestess. (She, meanwhile, has exited through the parodos by which she entered.)

When Orestes has set off for Athens, and Apollo has exited at the other side, the ghost of Clytemnestra can appear, mounting the ekkyklema from the shadowy doorway, to rouse the Furies; and these, when the ghost has retired, awake and descend, by twos and threes, to dance and sing in the orchestra, while the ekkyklema is withdrawn. (Although the Furies have been on stage since line *64* or thereabouts, their descent to the orchestra, starting at line *140*, stands as their proper entry, correctly introducing their first choral song). Apollo re-enters to drive the Furies from his precinct, which here includes the orchestra. When they have picked up the scent and chased off down the parodos, following Orestes, the platform can be rolled out again with the 'navel-stone' now replaced by a statue of Athene. This time the platform is extruded only far enough to suggest a shrine, resetting the scene as Athens for the remainder of the play.

From other plays it can be seen, for example, that when a specifically low entrance is required in *The Clouds* (see above, Ch.3) the platform could be rolled out to almost its full length, becoming, instead of steps up to a mansion, a dissociated rise in the street which nobody bothers to mention. Then, when Strepsiades is ordered to enter Socrates' house, whose lowliness is again emphasised, the rear steps are utilised: **'It looks to me',** he objects, **'like going down inside the cave of Trophimus'** (a notoriously deep and frightening cavern), and he and Socrates would be seen stooping and descending the ekkyklema's rear steps (*Clouds*, ll.507-8).

Again, I suggest that the ekkyklema would be the easiest and most convenient place for the suicide of Ajax. On or in the top can be set the socket which Ajax will need to hold his sword steadily point upward (**'The killer stands where it will cut most sharply... I have planted it carefully...'**) and the platform has been rolled halfway out, with the doors pulled back out of sight, turning it into a mere mound rather than a flight of steps, with the empty doorway leading into the imaginary 'wood' off-stage where soon Tecmessa will arrive, searching for her beloved master. Ajax, in utter despair, fixes his sword upright in the socket, and casts himself upon it;[49] he now lies there, in full view of the audience, but not of the chorus of sailors when they enter in two groups by the parodoi at either side of the orchestra. It is Tecmessa who finds him, crying out her grief off-stage when she first sights the body, before stepping forward on the platform to make her entrance and hold up her wide spread cloak, ostensibly to hide dead Ajax from all eyes[50] –**'He is not to be stared at!'** – but actually to let the actor, due shortly to reappear as Teucer, slip away unseen while an extra takes his place, or a dummy is substituted. So the ekkyklema can make Ajax' suicide easy, yet allow it to be far more effective than if carried out off-stage; it has also assisted Tecmessa to make an impressive entrance and then let her loving care of her master's body be clearly displayed to the audience.

I repeat that the convention is that of children at play; much is left to the imagination, guided by the actors' words, assisted by gesture and movement and the use of any prop that may be handy. Recalling the wooden box with which my brother and I played as children, which could be a ship, a house, a dungeon, a cave, a mountain, a car, train or plane, as occasion demanded, I cannot imagine the Greek dramatists having a property of so many possible uses as the ekkyklema without exploiting it to the full; and the texts themselves seem to hint at many such uses.

4

Dramatic Scenes in John's Gospel

The enduring quality of Greek tragedy is that the plays offer, as well as a full range of human weaknesses, noble moments when some person rises to extreme and costly unselfishness; and certainly the fourth evangelist was well versed in these. Within the novel which I have suggested as the Fourth Gospel's present genre, are found a number of dramatic passages which show striking resemblances to visual aspects of particular scenes, and others which echo the moral and emotional essence of scenes from the plays of Sophocles, Euripides or Aeschylus.

Visual Parallels

In John, when Jesus clears the temple he has a whip. This is perhaps envisaged as used only on the sheep and oxen, and not, as in El Greco's famous picture, on the traders also; but it is an addition to the Synoptic story. Imagined in dramatic terms, Jesus would make an entrance stage centre, through the double doorway, whip in hand. The whip recalls the well-known role of 'Whip-wielding Ajax', who enters (from the central doorway representing his tent or bivouac), carrying the most notorious whip in ancient drama, which he has used in a mad frenzy to scourge sheep and cattle (Sophocles, *Ajax*, 348-376). Since the Fourth Evangelist has deliberately introduced cattle and sheep (the Synoptics have only pigeons), for no other reason, it seems, than to show Jesus wielding that whip, it is likely that this plagiarism is intentional.

The reappearance of Lazarus, called out of his grave (11.38-44) is so nakedly dramatic that it is sensible to consider it as envisaged for a stage. Here the central doorway would make the entrance to the tomb of Lazarus; a tomb which, we are told, is a cave. Jesus orders it to be opened (**'Take away the stone!'**), two disciples would 'heave' open the doors, Jesus invokes his Father, and cries out with a loud voice, **'Lazarus, come forth!'** Then a chilling figure, **'bound hand and foot with grave-bands, and with a cloth over his face'** emerges, hobbling slowly until Jesus commands **'Unfasten him and let him go.'**

This would simply reproduce the return of Sophocles' doomed Philoctetes from the 'cave' into which he has withdrawn to await death (**'I shall go seek my father. Where? In Hades!'**) Neoptolemus, having tricked Philoctetes into lending him the bow, realises how shabby it would be to keep it, and, braving the fury of Odysseus and the Greek army, comes to restore to the lame archer the bow which will for him make the difference between death and life. Neoptolemus too stands near the 'cave-mouth', and he calls out **'Son of Poeas, Philoctetes I say, come out!'**. Then Philoctetes slowly emerges, hobbling on his agonising poisoned foot (Sophocles, *Philoctetes* 1209-62). The visual similarity needs no stressing; and was there any need for the explicit mention of Lazarus' tomb being a 'cave', except that the author had *Philoctetes* in mind?

A third important entrance in John is when the captive Jesus is brought back 'on stage' (John 19.1) -- or, as it is now written, out into the open forecourt in front of Pilate's Residency -- where the Judaeans (*hoi Iudaioi*) are waiting. Last seen normally dressed, Jesus now reappears as a shocking and pitiable figure, having already been stripped and flogged and then given a bright red cloak and a crown of thorns to mock his claim to kingship (John 19.1-5).

Now, as history, this is outrageous. That soldiers should tease and bully such a prisoner is all too likely, but that they should dare to send Jesus back to their commanding officer grotesquely garbed from their own barrack-yard foolery is simply not credible. In no army would this be seen as other than gross disrespect to their commander, and no governor conducting a public trial would tolerate being made a fool of by the lower ranks. Mark (15.15-20) has it correctly: the death-sentence is passed first; then the flogging, a standard part of the penalty for sedition, is administered, and after that the troops can have their bit of fun; but even so they put Jesus back in his own clothes before they produce him again in public.

The author, then, has altered the correct sequence to obtain his effect. Drama, after all, is not concerned with historical accuracy: what people will remember is the moving sight of the prisoner, keeping his dignity through pain and mockery, set there for all to see. '**Look at the man!**' says Pilate, ostensibly to the Judaean prosecutors, but really to the audience.

Why, further, does Pilate first re-enter by himself to announce that he is leading Jesus out for them to see? (John 19.4) This is again implausible since, even if Jesus was not to be flogged in public as Roman justice would expect, there was no need for Pilate himself to have escorted him inside (19.1); indeed, Pilate would have done better to remain and continue negotiating with the prosecuting Judaeans. It seems likely that the author had in mind here a famous scene of mockery in *The Bacchae*, when Dionysus enters first and only then calls forth Pentheus, a king driven mad and now dressed ludicrously as a woman, in order to expose him to ridicule; ridicule which can induce pity for that stupid, obstinate, but upright man, before Dionysus leads him away to his death.

Pentheus is the only character in the surviving plays to be so mocked on his way to a terrible end. This gospel's theology casts Jesus as a sacrificial victim, the Lamb of God. But in Greek tragedy the role of compliant and innocent sacrifice is usually female: Polyxena, daughter of Priam, who would rather die than be a slave; Iphigenia, who in the end dies for Greece and for Achilles; finest of all, Macaria, daughter of Heracles, who without hesitation goes to be sacrificed to save her family.[51] The doomed male is never slaughtered at the altar, and should go grandly, like Ajax, or Oedipus at Colonos, to his fated death. Pentheus alone is made ridiculous and so displayed.[52]

The connection here may seem less clear-cut than in previous examples, because Jesus would thus be combining two roles from *The Bacchae* -- Dionysus, the god-in-human-form-on-earth, and Pentheus, his hapless victim. However, as we shall see (below, Ch.6), the whole gospel is full of parallels with *The Bacchae*, which seem to put beyond question that the author had that play in mind when fashioning his own work and may have deliberately reshaped the Synoptic account of the soldiers' mockery of Jesus to resemble Dionysus' mockery of Pentheus.

Echoes

There are also many, possibly unconscious, echoes; that is, more subtle, non-visual parallels with the great tragedies. When Pilate, getting no answer, blusters, **'Are you not speaking to me? Surely you know that I have authority to release you, and authority to crucify you?'**, Jesus counters, **'You would have no authority over me at all, had it not been given to you from on high'** (John 19.10f).

When Creon, having established that Antigone knew of his edict that her brother's body was to be left unburied, then challenges: **'And yet you have presumed to break the law?'** she retorts:

> **Yes, for it was not Zeus proclaimed such things;**
> **and Justice, living with the Under Gods,**
> **did not appoint such laws for humankind.**
> **Nor did I think your edicts were so strong**
> **that a mere man should have his way, against**
> **the unwritten, changeless customs of the**
> **gods** (Sophocles, *Antigone,* 449-455).

Both prisoners are rejecting the Sovereign State, in the person of their judge, as final arbiter of right and wrong; well aware that to follow the higher loyalty will cost their lives.

Then there is the crucifixion tableau, with its dying hero central on his cross, flanked by his mother and the Beloved

Disciple.[53] This is one of John's great contributions to art. It is also absolutely against the practice of any army, let alone the disciplined Roman troops, to let friends and relatives attend, at close quarters, the public execution of a rebel;[54] but it makes an unforgettable scene. In the author's mind might be echoes of Aeschylus' crucified Prometheus, punished by merciless Zeus for having saved the human race from destruction; or Euripides' innocent Hippolytus, generously absolving his father of his death-guilt; but above all of Sophocles' dying Heracles, ensuring that the girl he loves will be looked after by his son (*Women of Trachis*, 1219-51). It is the parallel confiding by Jesus of his mother to the care of the favourite disciple ('**Woman, behold your son**', '**Behold your mother**') which is John's unique contribution to the death-scene (19.26f), and, imagined for a stage, it would demand that those playing mother and friend should stand within speaking distance of the cross, however unlikely that might be in real life.

Consider, too, the Easter morning scene between Mary Magdalene and the risen Jesus. Non-recognition is a commonplace of Greek theatre; but Mary's failure to recognise her master, whom she saw die, strongly echoes the failure of Sophocles' Electra to recognise her brother, whom she has just been told is dead. In neither case does the beloved, appearing unexpectedly, say in so many words, 'This is me. I am alive'; so flat a statement would detract from the dramatic moment of recognition. In each case, too, the woman, when overcome by emotion, is made to curb her outpouring of happiness because the man has unfinished business to complete. '**Do not cling on to me now**', says Jesus (John 20.17); '**Utter not the rest of the words**', pleads Orestes (*Electra* 1288).

Yet the Magdalene herself, as drawn by John, might owe more to the Antigone of Aeschylus' *Seven against Thebes*.[55] Unashamed to reject the city's authority and disobey, Aeschylus' heroine is no less independent than the one in Sophocles, no less determined, but more tender. The man '**the city hates**' she will honour with burial:

> **I, though a woman, will find a grave for him**
> **and earth for burial, which I will carry**
> **held in the lap of my long linen gown.**
> **I, I myself, shall cover him with earth,**
> **and none shall say me nay** (*Seven against Thebes*, 1043--6).

The prescribed rites are different, but Mary Magdalene's early morning venture to mourn 'the man the city hates' is emotionally exactly the same as Antigone's commitment:

> **If no one else will join his funeral,**
> **Myself I'll bury him and risk what comes**
> (*S.a.T*, 1033f).

The evangelist has sharpened the comparison by sending his Magdalene to the tomb unaccompanied by the other women.

Such parallels with the great classical dramas show that the Fourth Gospel was written by someone with, at the least, a wide knowledge and a love of the classical Greek theatre; and that dramatic and theatrical considerations stimulate the author's imagination, and shape his writing, to a noticeable degree. Such an author might have started out with the original intention of writing a play about Jesus.

5

Could A Christian Write A Play?

Precedent

Absurd though it may seem at first sight that any writer
from a first or second century Christian background could
even think of composing a drama about events in the life of
Jesus, there already existed several biblical plays. One, the
Exagōgē, by Ezekiel, a Jewish dramatist probably writing
at Alexandria during the second century BC, survives in
large part, telling the story of the Exodus, in Greek verse. It
was written for a Greek-speaking audience, perhaps with
the aim of presenting the Jewish people in a favourable
light compared with the Egyptians (Jacobson 1983, pp.1-
40). There is mention also of a *Susannah*, perhaps by
Herod's friend Nicolas of Damascus, who wrote tragedies
and comedies: and when a first century Alexandrian Jew,
Philo, in his *Life of Moses,* attacks authors who misuse
their education by writing comedies and licentious fables,
he is probably thinking of fellow Jews; for why should
he concern himself about a long-established habit of the
Gentiles? The *Exagōgē* by itself would in any case have
been precedent enough; and that work was still extant
when John was written, for we know it from the large
extracts quoted two centuries later by Eusebius in his
book *Praeparatio Evangelica.*

The prohibitions and denunciations of theatres by Clement and Tertullian (c.190–220 AD) imply that Christians less austere than they did indeed go to the theatre, and Tertullian's awful warning of a Christian woman who returned from the theatre 'possessed by the devil' makes it certain.[56] Nor was the writing of a play impossible, for in our author's time the precedent for basing a play on 'scripture' had already been set, so that a drama about the life of Jesus might well be within the capacity of a talented, educated Christian of the late first or early second century who possessed one or two of the Synoptic gospels.[57] Aristotle's *Poetics,* a treatise on the aims and practicalities of writing plays, would make an excellent guide for the beginner.

Purpose

What might a Christian author have hoped so to achieve? Greek tragedy

> **'is essentially the emotional response of its audience (...) And, most important of all, the affairs of the characters which move us are given a moral setting which is argued and explored in the play. They act and suffer within situations of moral conflict, of social, intellectual and theological conflict'** (Taplin 1989, p.169).

This is certainly crucial for John. From the Prologue, which sets out the fundamental theology and outlines the struggle to come, to that dramatic ending on the line, '**My Lord and my God!**', moral and theological considerations are expounded through the words and actions of the characters; so that abstract thought is given a concrete image with a strong emotional, as well as intellectual, impact. The Greek tragedians **'captured their audiences' minds, especially through their eyes'** (Taplin 1989, p.171). So it is in John: the word is made flesh, a principle is made manifest through human action, and we can see it, full of grace and truth; as one minor example may show. Mark records the *saying* that '**Whoever wants to be greatest must be the servant of all**'; but the Fourth Evangelist dramatises it, creating the unforgettable scene at the Last Supper where Jesus strips off his robe, girds himself with a towel, like a slave, and washes his followers' feet.

The scene is still powerful today. A modern Quaker calls it '**the sacrament of menial service, instituted by our Lord**'. As such it was, until the last century, re-enacted every Maundy Thursday, and still is, in many religious communities: but imagine it as acted before your eyes for the very first time. If this is fiction, it is great fiction, making real to the audience a great teaching. Given, therefore, that our author's self-declared purpose is to produce a work that will assist belief (John 20.31), it seems by no means impossible that he set out to *show* it as drama. To say that the author wrote as a dramatist is not to detract from this gospel, but to appreciate it better.

Implications

Many writers have commented on the dramatic quality of John's writing;[58] but to suggest that the first version of John really was the draft for a classical tragedy would increase existing doubts about its historical accuracy, since dramatists reshape history to make their plays. However, to consider the work as drama should make it easier to accept that entire episodes, some of which tax the belief of ordinary people, were indeed invented by the author. For the classical drama of Greece, known to the well-educated in the Roman empire as Shakespeare is to most of the English-speaking world now, did not simply narrate the story of, say, Agamemnon, or Prometheus. The Greek author would select, adapt and change the story, with even greater freedom perhaps than Shakespeare, bringing out whatever he saw as the key theme for his play.

For example, Aeschylus' *Libation-Bearers* and Sophocles' *Electra* both cover exactly the same ground; yet in one the recognition of Orestes by Electra comes early, in the other not until the play nears its climax. For the first is about the dilemma of Orestes, for whom the sacred duty to avenge his father means the unspeakable crime of killing his mother; while the second dwells on the sorrows of his loyal sister, changed at the last to overwhelming joy. Then Euripides quite drastically reinvents the same tradition in his *Electra*: focusing on the self-destructive nature of obsessional revenge, Euripides has Electra married off to a poor farmer, and Clytemnestra lured to Electra's cottage by a false message which plays on her maternal feeling, a humanity conspicuously lacking in the earlier Clytemnestras. In *The Phoenician Maidens* (they are temple-slaves at Thebes) Euripides, retelling the traditions already used by Aeschylus in *Seven against Thebes* and in the Theban plays of Sophocles, invents a plot quite incompatible with theirs.[59]

The dramatist must select, adapt, and invent, said Aristotle (*Poetics* 9.1-10). Our author was, I suggest, following Aristotle's advice. Modern playwrights do the same -- one need only compare Eliot's *Murder in the Cathedral* and

Anouilh's *Becket,* which present quite different Beckets. Both authors have treated the history loosely in order to communicate, in a moving and memorable form, by means of invented scenes, ideas important to themselves.

The Medium Shapes the Message

Even a playwright whose sole aim was to present 'the true facts' of a traditional story would be compelled to use the material creatively. No one, indeed, could have approached her theme more deeply convinced of its factual truth than Dorothy Sayers, writing *The Man Born to be King* in the 1940's; yet even so, as she explained, she found it necessary to create various minor characters, and to invent, for example, a sub-plot, involving Judas and her fictional 'Baruch the Zealot'.

She would have needed to alter more if her medium had been stage and not radio, and to invent more if she had only had Matthew, Mark or Luke to draw from; but, as she pointed out, **'when John is the authority for any scene, or when John's account is at hand to supplement those of the Synoptists, the playwright's task is easy'** (Sayers 1943, p.33). The remark was innocently intended, but perhaps that task was easy because it had already been done.

Basis for a Novel

Nor need it be very difficult to change play into narrative later; as Sayers herself did with *Busman's Honeymoon,* now best known as a novel, but originally written as a play.[60] The evangelist would have needed to extend his plot with a

Galilean Ministry (2.1-12; 4.1-54; 6.1-7.11) and to write into his script the place-names and times, descriptions of action, the explanation and the comment required by his new medium; while discarding or recycling the lines intended for the chorus. He could, and did, extend his narrative further by expanding speeches and controversies into the involved form which Kysar (1984 p.28) describes as **'spiraling'**, and adding whole chapters of 'discourse' to his Last Supper. (This was unfortunate, for his passion for saying everything again and again, with slight variations, makes controversy, such as the one which runs from 8.13 to 8.58, very tedious. After the original close to the Last Supper, signalled at the end of Chapter 14, there are now three verbose and mostly repetitive chapters, with only the occasional nugget of gold like 15.13, '**Greater love has no one…**').

For the novel the author would add 'introductions' or 'codas' to some scenes. He would complete his Passion story by restoring, embellished, versions of the Anointing at Bethany and Peter's Denial, scenes probably omitted from the play. He would also, it seems, compensate for the loss of dramatic effect when a play becomes a written narrative by adding in a mixture of hairbreadth escapes, disappearances and clandestine activity such as can be found in most of the ancient romances, and in John also; but not in the Synoptic tradition. Finally, he would add a chapter as epilogue, to make the more leisurely ending suitable for a novel.

Motives for Change

If it is asked why an author should transpose a work from one medium to another, one reason might have been that

John, like Cervantes, discovered that he was not a good enough poet to achieve success with a tragedy, and so turned to writing a novel; or perhaps he realised that a play about Jesus would never find a rich sponsor to back its production. A unstaged drama, too, would have a very small readership; a novel, likely to be more generally read, might be of greater help and influence within the church and might also reach farther outside. Possibly, again, the author, having created his characters, felt that he could do so much more with them if he moved beyond the constraints of the stage to the much wider scales of Place and Time and Casting available to a novelist. The mere thirst to imagine and create new episodes, like those of the Wedding at Cana and the Samaritan Woman, which are good stories but not suitable for stage production,[61] might have been reason enough. Perceiving such opportunities, what writer could resist?

It is, then, possible to imagine an early Christian wishing to write a play about Jesus, and later changing his mind, but that does not show that such a play was ever written. What may encourage us to seek further is that, as shown above in Chapter Two, the sole point of general agreement in serious studies of John is that there is ample evidence for an earlier version of some kind, probably documentary, behind the present gospel. Might not that first version have been a play?

6

Evidence For A Draft Play

Once the possibility has been envisaged that the original text behind the present narrative might have been a draft for a play, a great many aspects of John can be seen to point in that direction.

Unity of Place

A first requirement for a Greek play is that the action should be confined to one, or a very few, places – generally one place, though not perhaps closely defined; so that in *Ajax,* for example, the action, set in the Greek camp outside Troy, can drift from outside the hero's tent to the lonely shore where he commits suicide. Now in the Gospel of John the action is, to a remarkable extent, confined to the single location of Jerusalem. Out of the first twenty chapters of John (the whole of the book, apart from its epilogue), *only **Chapters Four and Six, (with short sections in five others)** are not set in Jerusalem or its immediate neighbourhood.*[62] (The contrast with the settings of the Synoptic Gospels, which range all over Galilee, into the territories of Tyre, of Philip's tetrarchy of Ituraea, into the Decapolis and lastly into Herod Antipas' other dominion of Peraea, east of the Jordan, before a single week constituting Jesus' only visit to

Jerusalem, is extreme.) This feature of John is, at the least, consistent with a dramatist, requiring Unity of Place for the drama of, say, *Jesus at Jerusalem*. Moreover, *all* these 'Jerusalem' incidents, public or private, spectacular miracles or narrow escapes, are, unless taken from the Passion Story itself, unknown to the Synoptics; which strongly suggests, especially when combined with the melodramatic nature of some scenes and the apparent impossibilities in others, that they may all have sprung from the writer's imagination.

Unity of Time

Aristotle's 'unities' were not the rigid principles later imposed on the French theatre, but rather an analysis of the factors which usually make a successful play. Just as Unity of Place means that most plays use a single, but quite flexible, location, so Unity of Time did not necessarily mean a single day; although, even when the logic of events reveals that two days, or a week, must have elapsed, this is not generally mentioned: the action continues, unbroken except by the chorus, one of whose functions is to allow time, unspecified, to pass while they sing.

Since a play cannot in any case attempt to show a whole life-story, but only a short period of crisis within that life, a dramatist would probably have based his play entirely on the final week of Jesus' life and presented a sequence of actions without reference to the passage of time; whereas a novel, relating but not showing the events, should be explicit, as the gospel now is, about times and dates. In this gospel John's highly dramatic version of the Cleansing of the Temple is now found at the start of Jesus' ministry, which quite contradicts the Synoptics; but as a scene for a play about Passion Week it would have come very near the beginning of that week, precisely where the Synoptics record it. Furthermore, from Chapter Seven to Chapter Twenty the whole action – if we ignore a suspense-heightening passage which moves Jesus to Transjordan and shows the disciples' reluctance to let him return to Judaea – would form a single sequence in time as well as in place, and could well result from an expansion of an original play-script which covered incidents, historical or imaginary, in Jesus' final week on earth.

Dramatic speeches

It is not only the restricted location and short, unspecific, span of time which suggest a play. Long speeches are not, in Greek literature, to be found only in drama; but an explanation for the extraordinary difference between the concise, aphoristic Jesus of Mark, and the self-proclaiming, almost flamboyant, Jesus of John can be found if the discourses and controversies in the fourth gospel are recognised as originally written as *speeches for the protagonist* (leading actor). Declaimed from a stage, both topic and style would be appropriate. '**The older poets make their characters speak like statesmen, and the modern ones like rhetoricians**' says Aristotle (*Poetics* 6.2).

However unnatural such speeches seem now, as part of a narrative, the transition from responsive answer to general declaration, apt to jar or puzzle a reader of the text, goes perfectly well on a stage. **'On what compulsion must I**?' snarls Shylock, only to have Portia launch into her Quality of Mercy speech; Nicodemus has only to ask, '**How can**

anyone be born when he is old? Can he go back into his mother's womb and be born again?', to cue a speech which, beginning from being born of the spirit, leads on with only the smallest prompt into enigmatic statements about coming down from heaven and being lifted up, culminating with '**Indeed, God so loved the world that he sent his only son...**' (John 3.1-21).

Much erudition has been expended to decide where in this third chapter of John we should insert the speech-marks which ancient texts did not use. How much of it is the direct speech of Jesus and how much is commentary by the author? On stage, either the actor, having begun by addressing Nicodemus, would turn to deliver the great message (3.16-21), ostensibly to the chorus but in fact to the audience; or, quite probably, the chorus themselves would take these lines. Neither way presents any difficulty to the spectator.

Use of 'I am'.

A further evidence of theatrical origin is that the speeches of Jesus are, in John, so notably egocentric. (The word is used here in its precise sense, meaning only that they are about Jesus himself.) Although this often goes unnoticed, when the words are heard in divine worship or studied for their theology, their egocentricity is exceptional. '**No one ever spoke like this**', say the temple officers (7.46); and in real life, no one does.

It is no accident that the word *eimi*, I am, occurs 54 times in John, almost five times the average figure for the other three gospels (Barrett 1978, p.6). Frequently in John *eimi* is emphasised with the unneeded pronoun *egō*; for example, when making the great claims that '**I am the bread of life**' (6.35), '**I am the light of the world**' (8.12), or '**Before Abraham was, I am**' (8.58). In just twelve verses, when speaking of the Door and the Good Shepherd (10.7-18), there are four instances of *egō eimi*, three of *egō* with other verbs and nine instances of words for 'me', 'my' or 'mine'. So the playwright can quite naturally present us with Jesus quite frequently alluding to himself in Greek which must remind his hearers of that name of God revealed to Moses. This covert suggestion of Jesus' own divinity is made very clear in the arrest scene, when the soldiers step back and prostrate themselves when Jesus answers '**I AM**'.

Now the stage is the one place where it does not seem unnatural to have a character hold forth at length about him or herself in a way which would sound odd in a book and preposterous in real life. Hamlet with his dilemma, Pentheus furiously indignant, Creusa lamenting her wrongs, Deianeira her luck, Ajax his shame and Hecabe her grief, all speak in the same theatrical mode. In terms of the medium, it makes no difference whether one is claiming to be the Light of the World or condemning oneself as '**a rogue and peasant slave**'; whether one admits to being '**subtle, false and treacherous**' or '**as normal as blueberry pie**'. Any such statement about oneself, especially when given at length, belongs only on the stage, where speech is the primary medium, and the actor is sharing his thoughts with each member of the audience. The declamations of Jesus, some unprompted, others arising in controversy, are highly theatrical and strongly support the suggestion of an original drafted play.

It might fairly be objected that the Bread of Life discourse (6.35-58), which is in precisely this egocentric style, could not, since it is set in Galilee, (6.59), have been part of a play set in Jerusalem; in which case the egocentricity would seem to prove only that all the speeches are in a rhetorical, but not in a specifically theatrical, mode. However, it is possible, even likely, that the Bread of Life declamation was originally written for the Last Supper scene in the play, but later repositioned in the novel to build theologically on the Loaves and Fishes miracle. There is definitely a clear difference between all such declamations and, for example, Jesus' conversation with the Samaritan woman (4.21-26), where he can speak of a high matter like true worship with no reference to himself, and where even the *egō eimi* when he proclaims himself Messiah fits naturally into the style of a normal conversation.

Thus the author did write in more styles than one, and when he was using a particularly theatrical mode he probably had a stage in mind. The one apparent exception, we have seen, might first have been written for his play, and later grafted into the Galilean scene. If briefer versions of the Bread of Life and True Vine speeches originally formed part of the Last Supper scene, to offer a theological interpretation of the eucharist, they may have been moved around to make way for the covert identification of the traitor (13.23-30); a scene that would seem ludicrous, like pantomime, if presented on the stage, but could have been added for a nice touch of cloak-and-dagger to the novel. The skilful adaption of an original passage to a new setting would account for both the overall unity of John ch.6, upheld by some critics, and the evidence for insertions detected in it by others (see Barrett 1978, pp.281-5). It can therefore be sustained that the style and tone of the speeches of Jesus point strongly towards an original dramatic script.

The Plot of a Play

The plot was 'the soul of tragedy', and the dramatist therefore even more a maker of plots than of verses (Aristotle, *Poetics*, 6.19; 9.9). A play must have a beginning, a middle and an end (*Poetics* 7.3). To set his play moving our author, after his prologue and opening chorus, would have a quick scene in which the Baptist heralds and identifies Jesus to his own disciples, and so also to the audience; then would follow the Cleansing of the Temple -- now, as in the Synoptics, the start to Jesus' Jerusalem activity -- leading at once to controversy with the chorus.

Next follow three miraculous cures at Jerusalem. '**The marvellous causes pleasure**', Aristotle maintains, but these have theological import, too, and are essential to the plot. The author has taken from Mark, and possibly from Luke, the themes of Healing the Lame, Curing the Blind and Raising the Dead, to construct a trio of increasingly marvellous cures *which would go well on stage*. The curing of a fever or the healing of a leper cannot easily be made effective spectacle, the multiplication of food or walking on water would be impossible to represent convincingly. Yet a paralysed man hoisting his bed on his back and walking away, a blind man who ceases to grope his way (or, like Tiresias, be led by a boy) but tosses aside his stick and dances off the stage, or the shrouded figure of a dead man appearing from his cavernous grave, these make good theatre.

Each theme could have come from Mark, and the unusual word *krabbaton* for bed and the use of spittle in a healing of eye-sight suggest that they did; but only details which suit the playwright's purpose are retained. (Just as carrying the bed demonstrated a cure, so spreading spittle over the eyes would display the healer at work). Each miracle leads to further controversy.

Play or no play, the similarities and differences between Mark and John are undoubted fact, and have given rise to speculation about an original, perhaps Aramaic, gospel, or 'Miracles' or a 'Signs Gospel'; theories which would now become needless. However, a very important change is from Mark's explicit and repeated foretelling by Jesus of his own death to John's almost unclouded climax of popular support as Jesus rides into the Holy City. The earlier hostility of crowds (John 5.18; 8.59; 10.32-9) has disappeared; the enemies plotting against Jesus (7.32, 45-52; 11.47-53, 57; 12.10) are powerless to act (7.45-9; 12.19); and throughout, Jesus has never given any but the most cryptic of hints about his own fate (3.14f; 7.33f; 8.21,28; 10.14-18; 12.7f., 32). Such an alteration would have been dictated by the requirements of a dramatic plot.

Mark relates the actual ride to the gates of Jerusalem as accompanied only by excited disciples chanting psalms; Luke and Matthew make the incident more impressive; but in John the author upgrades the spectacle further, places it after his dramatic Raising of Lazarus and asserts flatly that that tremendous miracle had led to many Judaeans putting their faith in him (11.45) and consequently to the temple hierarchy's resolution to have him put to death. The novel develops this theme with the Anointing at Bethany, and explains it in more detail; but in a play we would simply see Jesus enter, attended by cheering, palm-waving extras and half the chorus, to ride triumphantly all round the *orchestra*, well able to defy the evident hostility of the other half of the chorus who represent the authorities (see below, Ch.8); of whom the chorus leader, as 'High Priest', pronounces, with powerful dramatic irony, the 'prophetic' verdict that it was expedient for one man to die to avert the destruction of the nation.

Again, Mark's narrative has shown a long, slow progress, from Caesarea Philippi towards an inescapable, and repeatedly foretold, disaster at Jerusalem; but John introduces here a *peripateia*, that sudden, unforeseen, reversal of fortune which Aristotle says is the vital ingredient for the plot of a play (*Poetics* 6.17; 11.1). Jesus' now truly 'triumphal' entry into Jerusalem shows him at the height of his power, his enemies baffled and frustrated by his immense popular support; but soon comes the peripateia, his betrayal and arrest, leading to trial and crucifixion.

Even while they see Jesus at the crest of his popularity, the audience know how the story must end, just as they knew with Oedipus, Agamemnon or Antigone; but, for a moment, the author sweeps that knowledge away, as a good dramatist can,[63] with a loving Last Supper scene in which Jesus washes his disciples' feet. Then the doom begins, almost at once, with the Arrest; for neither the whispered scene in which Jesus reveals the traitor's identity, nor the long chapters of involved doctrinal discourse which follow, could belong to a play. Rather, the action would move on briskly from the close of the Footwashing (13.17), with not many more words before Jesus gets up and says **'Come, we must go from here'**(14.31), and then a few more lines spoken as he leads the disciples to another part of the stage, to reach 'Gethsemane' (18.1).

In a tragedy, location is not necessarily made specific. Jesus and his (two or three) disciples would have been seen to leave the 'supper room' (i.e., descend from the ekkyklema, which is then withdrawn), but their precise position when the arrest party found them was not important. In the narrative version an unnamed 'garden' is mentioned, for such a setting was too deeply entrenched in the tradition to be ignored, but John wastes no time there; even in that narrative, a single verse takes Jesus and his disciples to the garden, and two verses later Judas arrives with the arrest-party (John 18.1-3). The long, tormented wait at Gethsemane (Mark 14.32-41) has been cut, in the interest of *sudden* calamity.

The same dramatic urgency would explain the very short questioning of Jesus by 'the high priest Annas' (in the play, still the chorus leader, an unnamed priestly character) and the total absence of any proceedings before the Sanhedrin. The interrogation of Jesus by Caiaphas in Mark 14.53-64 becomes, in the Fourth Gospel, a mere token appearance (18.19-23), which in the play would have had no place at all. For it would be important for the playwright to move the action briskly from Arrest to Trial, and it would not make good theatre for one trial scene to follow another. Jesus is brought straight from 'Annas' to Pilate and then suspense is maintained by Pilate's attempts throughout the trial to effect Jesus' release; but the pressure on the governor, from the whole chorus, mounts steadily, until finally Jesus is condemned. The plot is structured not merely to narrate, but to make an audience feel, the pathos of the hero's downfall.

Yet the life and death of the human Jesus do not make up the whole of John's plot. Aristotle had observed that a tragedy must not show well-deserving men going from good fortune to bad (*Poetics* 13.2); nor do the gospels end at Jesus' death. The reappearance scenes with Mary Magdalene and Thomas are not a bolted-on happy ending, they are the essential completion of the plot that was outlined in the prologue. In theological terms, the divine Word is made human flesh, thus losing his invulnerability although not his other divine powers. He comes, unrecognised, to his own people and is rejected by all but the few; yet in the last act, after his sufferings, he is vindicated, acknowledged by his Father and restored to glory, and the faithful few worship and rejoice. The summary given in the prologue and the repeated claims put into the mouth of Jesus of a special relationship with the Father (e.g. John 5.17-29) leave no doubt that this pattern is a deliberate creation: if Jesus' intransigent demand for men's allegiance inevitably leads, at the human level, to his death, it is the same intransigent claim to divine authority which makes the resurrection an equally inevitable consequence, on the cosmic plane.[64]

John and The Bacchae

It has been mentioned above that the outlines of plot in the prologues of *John* and of *The Bacchae* are closely parallel. So are their plots in full. In *The Bacchae* too, the god on earth goes unrecognised in his human form, in spite of overt miracles and cryptic hints. In both works the refusal of some to acknowledge the hero's divine authority leads to terrible suffering. Dionysus vows to avenge the insult (*Bacchae 850*). Jesus is no less sure of the doom of those who reject or oppose him (John 8.21-26; 9.36ff; 12.31, 35,48f). During the play Jesus alone is seen to suffer, undergoing not only arrest and captivity, like Dionysus, but also ridicule and agonising death, like Pentheus; but the calamities which will later punish those who rejected him are clearly foreshadowed (11.47-50), and an audience could not fail to remember that total disaster had followed for Jerusalem, in 70 AD[65]. Pentheus' obstinate opposition to Dionysus brings ruin on the house of Cadmus; the rejection of Jesus will lead to nothing less than the destruction of priesthood, temple, city and nation.

Each play ends with an epiphany of the divine protagonist, his human disguise discarded. In *The Bacchae* this allows the god to pronounce the future sufferings of Agave and Cadmus, but in John, where the divine hero has suffered so much, it seals a happy ending as his faithful friends discover and acknowledge his true identity – **'My Lord and my God!'**

This final *peripateia* in John, the Resurrection, does indeed belong to the Synoptic story; but whereas in Matthew and Luke a vision of angels at the tomb is only a prelude to a subsequent meeting with the risen Jesus elsewhere, the version in John is made more sudden and much more effective, with no time wasted between Mary's brief encounter with angels and her meeting with Jesus himself (John 20.11-18).

Three significant elements of the Synoptic Passion scenario are entirely omitted from the Gospel of John: the clear predictions earlier of Jesus' death, the Sharing of the Bread and Wine (Mark 14.22-5), and the agonised Waiting for Arrest at Gethsemane (Mark 14.32-42); furthermore, the proceedings before the high priest are short and futile, and the Sanhedrin is never mentioned. These omissions cannot properly be ascribed to ignorance: reasons have already been given to suppose that the author was in fact very well acquainted with those earlier gospels, however freely he might use them. One may choose to conjecture theological motives for the omission from John of what are integral elements of the Passion in Mark; but the need for a dramatic *peripateia* in the plot is a sufficient explanation by itself. The suggested outline given above fully meets the criterion of a 'sequence of scenes arising probably or necessarily from each other', leading from a clear beginning to a definite end (*Poetics* 7.12).

It would also offer a satisfactory suggestion for a first draft – satisfactory because there could be obvious motives, first for writing it and then for changing and amplifying it, with the distinct possibility that an author, eager now to produce a novel, might fail to make seamless joins and logical transitions as he expanded his scenes or added new incidents. The greater part of the gospel which we have today consists of material with at least the potential to form the plot and dialogue of a complete drama; missing only a number of passages for the chorus. That almost all the sections which would fit suitably into a play either have no precedent in the Synoptic tradition, or else diverge markedly from it, supports the likelihood that they are the author's own creation. This would be perfectly consistent with the suggestion that the writer first drafted his own play and later incorporated it into a historical novel; a transformation which is not only feasible, but which would explain many puzzling features found in the text as we have it today.

7

Theatrical Scenes

Written for the Theatre

Already varied evidence has been offered to suggest that
the first version of the Gospel of John may have been the
draft for a Greek tragedy: dramatic scenes reminiscent of,
or derived from, the great Athenian plays and a prologue
in the style of drama; dramatic scenes at Jerusalem which,
in the same order in which they now appear in the gospel,
could make a virtually complete play; alterations to the
storyline of the Synoptic gospels required in order to
contrive a suitably dramatic plot, and the alteration of the
Synoptic Jesus into an egocentric declaimer better suited
for a stage. A *prima facie* case has been presented.

There are, however, scenes which provide stronger
evidence, being designed apparently to obtain visual effects
which would be useful or even striking in a theatre, but
which in the narrative seem pointless, or pass unnoticed.

It need not be thought that a concern for visual effect is
anachronistic. The poet should keep the stage (*skēnē*)
'before his eyes', said Aristotle, listing visual effect (*opsis*)
among the four main ingredients of drama (*Poet*.17.1,
18.7b). Reference has been made above to visual effects

apparently borrowed from classical plays, such as Jesus with a Whip in the temple (cf. Mark 11.15-19) or Jesus, pitiable and ludicrous in robe and 'crown' of thorns, led out by Pilate (cf. Mark 15.16-20). But in a number of other instances, in each of which the author of John deviates from Mark and the Synoptic tradition, his version is not only more dramatic, but more theatrical; that is, it has features *which are only effective, or only intelligible, if such scenes were originally drafted with stage production in mind.*

Stage Effects

There are six obvious examples in the narrative, each one inconsistent with Synoptic tradition, and all, in the present narrative form, illogical and unnecessary:

i). The Pool of Siloam

The healing technique used on the Blind Man (John 9.1-12) is unique in the New Testament, for he is sent away, with clay-daubed eyes, to effect the cure at the pool *in the absence of his healer.*[66] This use of clay, mixed with spittle, seems to derive from the use of spittle in healing the blind man in Mark 8.23b; clay might be added by John to make the effect more visible, and make a good excuse to send this blind man to tap his way slowly to a property 'pool' or fountain-basin against the skene wall. There, under pretext of washing off the clay, he would be able to alter the eyes of a special mask from 'blind' to 'seeing' before facing round to astonish the audience.[67]

Now, in the narrative version, the Pool of Siloam serves no purpose, for the rest of the story would follow equally well if

Jesus had cured the man on the spot (cf. Mark 8.22-6; 10.46-52) and sent him home; but if the scene was first drafted for the theatre, then the trip to the 'pool' not only makes the visual mechanics of the 'cure' simple, but also builds up suspense while the audience wait to see what will happen. If this scene had first been written to be read, such mechanics would not have been needed; it is only when it is imagined as on a stage that the pool is both logical and necessary.

ii). **Mourners from Jerusalem**

Also improbable are the many people who arrive -- from Jerusalem, less than two miles away -- three days too late for the burial when they come to comfort Lazarus' sisters (11.18f). They have no significant role, merely following Mary to the tomb and commenting on the action (11.36f). (Later they tell John's sinister 'Pharisees' about it; but one passerby or simply, as in 4.1, '**When the Pharisees had heard**', could have done that equally well.) Yet, if imagined as the chorus of a play, who move processionally, singing a lament, joined in this by Mary and Martha from the stage itself, their presence would have purpose and impact; their later comments would also fit the role of chorus, and the fact that they have come long after the burial would pass unnoticed in production. Such a scene is clearly envisaged by Aristotle when he defines a *kommos* as '**a dirge shared** (*i.e. sung alternately*) **between the chorus and** [*actors singing*] **from the stage**' (*Poet*.12.9).

iii). **The Soldiers**

Then there are the soldiers at Gethsemane (18.3), who in reality could only have been Roman auxiliaries under the command of the governor, since those were the only troops in Judaea, and the narrative is speaking of a large body of men (*speira* equals company, or even battalion). In terms of history, no sensible governor would risk igniting revolt among the Passover pilgrims by the obvious provocation of sending out such a force of Roman troops to arrest a popular prophet, since they could not possibly move secretly through the overcrowded city, even by night.

It has been argued that the evangelist is so determined to lay all responsibility on the Jews that he would never have introduced Roman soldiers had they not been part of the tradition; and the council's statement (John 11.48) that, if Jesus is not dealt with, '**the Romans will come and sweep away our temple and our nation**' is supposed to support this (Winter 1961, pp.44-50). Yet this last verse, written after the Romans had indeed destroyed temple and nation in 70 AD, is better taken as dramatic irony; the author reminding his audience of the terrible disaster which, as he sees it, came upon the nation, not because they failed to suppress Jesus, but because they succeeded.

The real motive for the presence of soldiers is their theatrical effect. Armoured and helmeted figures are intrinsically menacing, and four or even two helmeted 'soldiers' would lend impact to the arrest scene, whether their presence were historically credible or not. The lanterns and torches (18.3), another detail found only in John, have been interpreted symbolically (Barrett 1978, p.519), but make better sense as stage props to show that the arrest is taking place at night. The binding of Jesus' hands (18.12), which in Mark does not take place until he is to be marched through the streets next morning (Mark 15.1), is a final touch to emphasize visually how completely the hero is now in the power of his enemies.

The colonel (*chiliarch*) (18.12), appropriate only if this squad really is a whole battalion, suggests an author not versed in military niceties, writing a connecting passage for his narrative in, one must admit, a rather careless style.

iv). **The Trial**

The Trial by Pilate has often been noted as dramatic, but when it is seriously envisaged as action on a stage a great many vexed problems are solved. The unconvincing excuse that the Judaeans would not enter the Residency (which they had no need to do, trials being held outside, in public) to avoid ceremonial defilement, seems to be simply the novelist's subsequent rationalisation of the fact that the whole scene is played with Pilate and the prisoner on stage, and the chorus, whether taking the part of the chief priests as accusers or of the crowd calling of Jesus' crucifixion, below, in the *orchestra*.

(We may suppose that the accusation would have been made first by the 'priestly' half-chorus, even though even the narrative makes little mention of chief priests here. At the start the accusers are only 'they' (John 18.28), and then *hoi Judaioi*; for during the course of the trial the entire chorus becomes vehemently hostile.)

Pilate's dilemma is visually illustrated as he repeatedly comes forward to address the chorus and then retreats to question his prisoner. One result of this continual to-and-fro may be the little aporia at 19.9, where the novel makes Pilate re-enter the Residency to speak to Jesus, forgetting that Jesus has already been brought out after his flogging to be displayed to his accusers (19.5), so should still be standing out there -- at the back of the stage, in theatrical terms. In the later narrative, at 19.13 Jesus is now brought out again, although there has been no mention of his being taken back inside first.

The claim that Pilate had Jesus flogged while still hoping to release him has usually been recognised (Barrett 1978, 540f) as being for the sake of the dramatic effect of bringing that bleeding, grotesquely garbed figure out on display, because in any other terms his action is quite pointless. Since nothing could be farther from the author's mind than historical accuracy, it is almost certain that the ambiguous *ekathisen* ('seated himself' or equally 'seated him', John 19.13) meant that Pilate now seated Jesus on the official seat of judgement, to display him to his prosecutors. Not credible as history, but again fine dramatic irony, since the prisoner in the judge's seat will one day return to judge the world; and a visually effective piece of theatre.

In the end Jesus is handed over to 'them' to be crucified (19.16). For 'them' here still to mean the Judaeans, the chorus down in the orchestra, would be impractical in the theatre, as well as historical nonsense. Here 'them' must mean the two armed and helmeted extras up on the stage, who have escorted the prisoner ever since his arrest and now lead him inside to meet his doom. The verbal confusion can be accounted for if the author, having created this scene for a stage, had it still before his eyes when writing his novel and did not notice that what is obvious to an audience might not be so clear to his reader.

v). **The Crucifixion**

Yet another departure from Synoptic tradition is the emphatic statement that Jesus carried his cross all the way:

'**And carrying his cross himself** (*heautō*, for himself) **he went out to the Place of the Skull... There they crucified him**' (19.17f). This makes the Johannine narrative gospel less striking than the vivid tale of the conscripting of Simon of Cyrene (Mark 15.21), which also gives Mark's reader a stark impression of the state to which Jesus had been reduced by a particularly brutal flogging. But if the author was envisaging stage production, then his big scene would have required Jesus, with a beam of wood lashed across his shoulders, escorted by four soldiers (cf.19.18), forming a procession to enter at one side of the *orchestra* and, to the music of a solemnly sung chorus, to climb to the stage by the ramp at its end to reach 'Golgotha'. There Jesus must climb again, onto the ekkyklema. This is now fitted with an upright for the cross, to which his crossbeam will be fastened; and there he will stand as the clear focal point for this climactic scene.

A play would certainly have omitted the two robbers, because a stage with three crosses would have looked, and been, cluttered. Four extras are already needed as soldiers; to add more as the thieves would merely lessen the visual effect of the lone man carrying his cross, and detract from the big scene between Jesus and his disciple and mother. Further, the play would have been slowed down by the need to remove their bodies, and their crosses, from the stage. Now, in John's narrative, the thieves say nothing, and appear to have no purpose except to comply with tradition; which is at least consistent with their having originally been omitted entirely from an earlier version.

Four soldiers, as specified in the text,[68] are a ludicrously inadequate force from an army of occupation to stand guard over the execution of a national in any occupied country, especially one who was yesterday a popular hero;

and still less when the guards sit around dicing. For a stage-army, however, a small number is inevitable and four would, in fact, look appropriate on a stage.

The scene with Jesus' mother and the beloved disciple has been mentioned already as another historical impossibility, introduced for theatrical reasons. Replacing Mark's despairing '**My God, my God, why did you desert me?**', in Aramaic, and the loud shout with which Jesus dies (Mark 15.34,37), with '**I thirst**' and '**It is accomplished**', in Greek (John 19.28, 30), the author simplifies language and clarifies thought, consistent with the needs of stage production. Theatrical also is the spear-thrust, a visual corroboration of 'death' necessary here, before the 'corpse' is removed; but the 'relevant' biblical quotations would have been added later for the novel.

The burial by Joseph of Arimathea and Nicodemus (19.38--42) is another embellishment which must have been written in later. To begin with, there is no dialogue; and even though that could have been be covered by the chorus, stagecraft forbids the introduction at this point in the play of two almost unknown characters merely to carry off a corpse; the withdrawal of the ekkyklema, bearing cross and victim, and followed by the soldiers, would be much simpler. The burial episode was written to be read, not for production. In a play, anything which needed to be known about the burial of Jesus could better have been told in monologue by Mary Magdalene at the opening of the next scene.

vi) **The Resurrection**

Of the last two chapters of John, Chapter 20 is predominantly novel material and Chapter 21, described earlier as an epilogue, is exclusively so. If Mark ever related appearances of the risen Jesus these would probably have been simpler versions of those now found in Matthew, whereas here the author seems to prefer Luke for his Male Disciples Visit the Tomb story (John 20.2-10; cf. Luke 24.24) and the Appearance Indoors (John 20.19-23; cf. Luke 24.36-49). However, John's two most original appearances, to Mary Magdalene at the Tomb and to Doubting Thomas, could well have formed the closing scenes of a play: Mary meets Jesus, then reappears to tell the disciples, with Thomas refusing to believe it until the Risen Jesus suddenly is there.

Both are highly dramatic episodes. In the first, a 'non-recognition' scene such as Greek dramatists often employed, what most strongly suggests theatrical practice is the much debated line, '**Do not cling on to me, for I have not yet gone to the Father**' (20.17). Speculation as to the theological implications of this incomplete stage of resurrection has been matched by ingenious suggestions for emending the text; but stagecraft offers a straightforward answer: Jesus cannot yet have ascended to glory, *because he is still wearing his ordinary clothes.*

For non-recognition, the scene demands that the risen Jesus must still be in everyday clothes, so that he can be mistaken for a gardener (20.14ff). Yet in his final apotheosis, at which the mere sight of him must reveal his supernatural status not only to Thomas but to a whole audience, Jesus must wear the dazzling robes appropriate to any supernatural being: that is a convention which appears in the synoptic gospels, in Josephus' history, in the ancient novels, in the apocryphal *Gospel of Peter*, in fact anywhere in the whole ancient world.[69] The author of

John has therefore concocted a neat explanation to prepare the audience for a second resurrection appearance which will be strikingly different from the first.

In his narrative John is able to stress repeatedly that Jesus enters through closed doors (20.19, 26b); but on stage, however the sudden appearance of Jesus might be contrived, a shining white or brilliantly coloured robe would be *de rigeur* to befit this epiphany. Jesus cannot appear 'above' the stage, on the theologeion which topped the skene, where a divine personage might be expected, since he must offer to let Thomas feel his hands and his side; and so his recognition as a divine being, which is the final climax of the plot announced in the prologue, would largely depend on his sudden appearance in 'divine' clothing. Theatrical presentation thus offers a practical explanation for a very puzzling verse: '**I have not yet gone to the Father**' in the recognition scene (20.17) is simply a line to account for the resurrected Jesus not yet being arrayed in the 'robes of glory' which he merits, and in which he will next appear.

The nails, which figure in all crucifixion art but nowhere in the Synoptic accounts, are never, even in John, mentioned until the uncompromising challenge by Thomas: '**Unless I see in his hands (or wrists) the mark of the nails and put my finger into the mark of the nails (...) I will not believe it**' (20.25b). It may be that the idea of the *nailing* of the hands only occurred to the author when writing this scene, in which nail-wounds on the palms of the actor's hands would indeed be far more effective visually than rope-marks on his wrists, or wounds in side and feet which his robes would hide.

Verbal Scene Setting

At the start of any scene on the flexible Greek stage, although at times some prop may suggest, e.g., a shrine or a tomb, any more precise information needed by the audience must be conveyed in speech. Tiresias, for example, manages in four lines to identify himself, his exact location, and the actor next to appear: '**Who's on *the gates*? Summon from his dwelling Agenor's son, *Cadmus*, who, leaving Sidon, fenced this *city of Thebes* with towers. Go, somebody, and let him know *Tiresias* seeks him**' (*Bacchae* 170-173).[70]

In John, lines which might have been designed to inform an audience may be found in:

i) *Three healings.*

The need to inform an audience would account for some unnecessary questions. On seeing the Blind Man the disciples ask '**Master, who sinned, this man or his parents, for him to be born blind?**' (9.2); but neither question nor answer serve any purpose in the story. An audience, however, although mask, staff and movements show them that the man is blind, must be told that he has been so afflicted from birth, in order that this healing shall seem an unprecedented marvel (9.32).

Even odder is the question given to Jesus himself when he sees a paralysed man at a known place of healing (5.6). '**Do you want to be cured?**' seems, in the circumstances, somewhat crass and insensitive; but, as the sick man's cue to explain his condition, it would be perfectly natural. The start of the verse, '**When Jesus saw him and knew that

he had been lying there a long time' suggests that Jesus may, in an earlier draft, have asked him first how long he had been there, drawing the attention of the audience both to the location at Bethesda and to the severity of the affliction.

In the third dramatic healing, that of Lazarus, both his sisters identify themselves to the audience by their (identical) words to Jesus, '**Lord, if you had been here,** *my brother* **would not have died.**' Martha later supplies the fact that Lazarus has been dead four days, making this another unprecedented miracle.

ii) *The Levite's question.*

When Jesus appears briefly before Annas -- or Caiaphas, following the minority reading; but no name would be required in a play -- the question **'Is that the way to answer the high priest?'** (18.22) confers a specific, if temporary, identity on the leader of the chorus. (Since this short episode does nothing to further the plot, it may only be another sop to tradition, added later during the rewriting; but it might possibly have been written into a play to give the actor playing Peter more time to change from his 'disciple' costume into a toga or a military outfit, with a different mask, before reappearing as Pilate.)

iii) *Angels at the tomb.*

The angels in the scene with Mary Magdalene might also be thought a sop to tradition, for they do nothing, except to ask her why she is weeping; which is her cue to inform the audience by answering that her master's body has disappeared. But in the gospel as it now stands, this is already known from 20.2, where she has told Peter and the other disciple. In a play, on the other hand, the scene would begin with Mary entering alone, lantern in hand, announcing that she must go to the tomb while it is still dark (20.1) and then seeing that the 'tomb' has been 'opened'; she would need her angelic interlocutor so that the audience may learn what she has failed to find there. An inconsistent expansion of an original theatrical scene in which the male disciples did not appear would account both for the virtual repetition of Mary's statement about the body (20.2, 20.13b), and for the fact that the angels, sitting in the tomb, were not seen by the men; who also seem to ignore Mary when she has arrived back at the tomb (20.10f).

A Limited Cast

Greek plays, developing from a choral form, had only gradually worked up to using as many as three actors, and never went further, although occasionally there is a fourth person who has a line or two – perhaps an extra with a good voice.[71] With such insignificant exceptions, the speaking roles were shared between three actors, changing masks and voices as needed. When acting became, in the Hellenistic period, an organised profession, each troupe had three actors only, so our author would never have considered any larger number.

The effects of this tiny cast can often be seen. In Sophocles' *Electra*, for example, the leading actor plays the title role, the second man is both Orestes and Clytemnestra, while the third man does the small parts of Old Servant, Electra's Sister, and Aegisthus. As a result, Orestes' loyal companion Pylades, indispensable to the tradition, is only a walk-on part for the extra, without a line to say.[72] There can never be more than three persons with speaking parts on stage at one time; often there will be fewer, while one, or possibly two, actors are changing for other roles. In John, The Raising of Lazarus appears to be limited by just such a restriction to the number of actors.

Lazarus

The story as it stands ends too abruptly, as the literary critics point out.[73] It would have been sensible, and in the usual pattern of miracle stories, to have the risen Lazarus not only appear but also speak, like Luke's young man at Nain, thus proving himself fully alive. Dorothy Sayers found it expedient for her Lazarus to speak when he appeared; and while her medium of radio would naturally make a vocal Lazarus desirable, she went further, exploiting the theological possibilities of a character returned from the dead (Sayers 1943, pp.201, 214ff; notes pp.209ff.). The author of John might have been glad to do the same, and should at least have made the 'dead' man say something, had he not been composing this scene for the theatre; but with three actors already on stage as Jesus, Martha and Mary, Lazarus could not be more than a walk-on part for an extra.

(Euripides had faced a rather similar problem in *Alcestis* (1144ff), and his heroine, brought back to the land of the living by Heracles, has not a word to say to her beloved husband. The *pretext* is that she must for three days remain silent, until released completely from the power of the underworld; the *reason* is that the leading actor, who plays Alcestis, also plays Heracles; so that in this final scene it is an extra, wearing the mask and robe of Alcestis, who is led back in silence to her husband by the mighty son of Zeus.)

The evangelist could have changed the ending of the Lazarus scene for his novel, but was perhaps more concerned to maintain pace by moving on to the prophecy of Caiaphas, which he now amplifies (11.51ff). He then underlines the theme of danger by moving Jesus away from Jerusalem again, explains how **'the chief priests and Pharisees'** are watching out for him, and stresses support for Jesus with the Anointing at Bethany episode, before rejoining the plot of his tragedy for the triumphal procession. In the narrative version, the 'reality' of Lazarus' restoration to life is shown by having him host the dinner-party at Bethany, and so the novelist avoided having to tinker with the end of his dramatic 'raising from the dead' scene.

Judas

With only three actors, the Greek dramatists had to limit severely the total number of speaking parts in the whole play, as well as the number on stage at one time; which probably explains another puzzle. Although in Mark the treacherous Judas comes to greet Jesus as '**Master**' and kiss him, with Luke adding the telling line, '**Judas, would you betray the son of man with a kiss?**', this highly emotive incident is omitted in John, and Judas plays no active part here. Having brought a squad of soldiers and temple police to the garden (18.3), he merely '**stood there with them**' (18.5b).

Which is odd, considering the trouble taken earlier in John to build up an unsympathetic and sinister picture of Judas

(6.70f; 12.6; 13.21-30), culminating when Jesus at the Last Supper indicates him to the favourite disciple as the traitor (13.24ff). Judas' final appearance, at the garden, is, in John, barely mentioned, a complete anticlimax. However, the planted clues to Judas' lack of integrity, and the covert signalling of the traitor (13.21-9) are unsuitable for a stage and can only belong to the novel. A playwright would have omitted Judas completely from the play, perhaps leaving an extra to walk on with a lantern as a nameless guide for the menacing, helmeted soldiers.

As novelist, the author has brought his portrait of a traitor to a climax with Judas receiving the morsel from the hand of Jesus and at once departing to effect the betrayal: '**He went out. And it was night.**' Tradition insisted that Judas must now be named as bringing the arrest-party to the garden; but to have allowed him to go further and personally identify Jesus, as he does in the Synoptics, would have destroyed the dramatic '**I AM**' declaration, which depends on Jesus having to identify himself. This scene, showing Jesus both as the human leader nobly sacrificing himself to protect his followers (18.8), and also, like Dionysus in *The Bacchae*, offering a strong hint of his divine identity, so nearly explicit that the audience must be amazed that his captors fail grasp it, was too good to jettison. At the garden, therefore, the briefest mention of Judas served best.

The Thieves

Similarly, the two thieves would, as we have seen above, have been eliminated from the Crucifixion scene; for when, to placate tradition, they are restored in the novel, they have nothing to do or say. On a stage they would have blunted the clear visual effect of Jesus flanked by his mother and favourite disciple; and anyway, four extras are already required, as the execution squad dicing for Jesus' clothes (John 19.23).

Mary Magdalene alone.

That the writer brings Mary Magdalene to the tomb *by herself* is as much dramatic as theatrical: one lone woman daring to visit the condemned man's tomb is a more powerful image than when several do so. Moreover, the non-recognition scene, so beloved by Greek dramatists, might lose credibility and impact if other women were with her; but further, cost, if nothing else, limited the number of extras available, while unnecessary characters would clutter both stage and plot. When recasting his play into a novel the author might as easily have returned to the tradition and included the other women, and then, when they all ran in panic (Mark 16.8a), have sent Mary on her own to tell Peter and the other disciple (John 20.2); but probably he thought, quite rightly, that his non-recognition scene was too good to alter, and so let it stand.

The Twelve

In a play it would have been neither practical nor artistically sound to provide Jesus with twelve disciples, crowding the stage and spoiling the spectacle. Two, perhaps three at the most, of whom only 'Peter' and 'Thomas' speak, would be realistic. Even in the existing narrative the Twelve get only four mentions,[74] and not one in any line suggested as part of the play. There is one reference to the Twelve as a unit (6.67); the others emphasize membership of the chosen group as accentuating the iniquity of treachery or the folly of doubt. It would have sounded foolish to speak of twelve disciples on a stage where so few can be deployed.

Theatricality

The theatrical nature of these instances may be seen more clearly by comparison with other parts of the gospel. The author had an active visual imagination, whatever his medium. When he is writing narrative, '**So Jesus, tired by his journey, sat down on the well. It was about noon**' (4.6), for example, gives a clear sketch of the traveller, tired, hot and thirsty under the noonday sun; it is vivid, but not dramatic. The exit of Judas from the Last Supper, '**Then, having accepted the morsel, he went out. And it was night.**' (13.30), is striking and dramatic, but it is not practical theatre: for the effect would be lost in the outdoor, day-lit, classical theatre, and so must come from the novelist. Similarly, the grave-clothes in the tomb, with '**the face-cloth, wound together, lying separately**' (20.6,7), are visually memorable as described but not effective on the stage; for most of the audience sat too far away (hence those larger than life-size masks) and such wrappings could appear at best as a white blur, conveying no obvious message.

The retention elsewhere of theatrical effects is strong evidence for the fourth gospel having begun as the draft for a tragedy. For these instances explain hitherto irrelevant or perplexing details in the narrative as effects which would be striking and appropriate on stage; but which lose force or pass unnoticed in the novel. (The final scene with Thomas is an exception, for it remains striking and theatrical even as narrative.) They contrast sharply with visual effects in other parts of the gospel which are clearly designed to convey a sharp image to a *reader* and those who hear him.

We have noted also the use of 'scene-setting' questions, which now appear redundant; the silence of Lazarus; the scanty references to The Twelve, which have led some scholars to suppose that in this tradition the disciples numbered only seven; the insignificant roles of the sinister and villainous Judas at Gethsemane, and of the thieves at the crucifixion. All these make sense in terms of casting and staging a play. It seems most likely that many scenes in the gospel were first drafted with stage-performance in the author's mind.

8

The Chorus

The Roles of the Chorus

The chorus was the bedrock of Greek tragedy, being the source from which all drama had developed; Walton sees the origin of the actor in the solo work of a bard, interacting with his chorus. The chorus itself has two distinct roles. In one it can sing of the griefs, mistakes and troubles of particular people, and set these in the universal context of the gods and their dealings with humanity; **'it is... the place of choral song to move into a different world, a different register, distinct from the specific events of the plot'** (Taplin 1989, p.13). In its other mode, however, at other times, the chorus may often be involved in the dialogue, with its leader, or the whole chorus (sometimes in two groups), involved in the plot to the extent of advising, pleading, sympathising with or condemning the principals; even, in *The Libation-Bearers* (770 - 82), ensuring Aegisthus' death by persuading the Old Nurse to alter Clytemnaestra's message. Of this mode Aristotle says that **'The chorus must be considered as one of the actors... and should take part in the action'** (*Poetics* 18).

The chorus does not need to show consistency. For example, in Sophocles' *Antigone* the substance of the choral passages is sublime, singing of the great power of man, used for good or evil, or of the harshness of fate on the unfortunate; yet in dialogue the chorus of elderly men show themselves all too human - sycophantic, doddery, superstitious, male-chauvinist, ready with good advice when it is too late. Nor need a chorus, in either role, have only a single point of view: in 'universal' mode they may, singing in two halves, turn and turn about, express differing views; as part of the action, they may be sharply divided, and express individual opinions. If we think of them in their first mode as the inspired voice of the bard, able none the less to see both sides of a question, and in the second mode as the voices of public opinion, expressing different and shifting viewpoints, then both roles are easily understood.

So we must **'approach the chorus with an extremely flexible notion of identity'** (Rehm, p.59); that is, they need not always seem just like the same people whom we last heard. In our suggested play the chorus would sing some great hymnlike passages expounding the play's cosmic meaning; yet they are also the argumentative hearers of the protagonist's speeches and, in the trial scene, his accusers; they would mostly take the role of antagonist, as do the chorus of Furies in Aeschylus' *Orestes*. They would, too, comment on the actions of the hero, very likely with divided opinions, strophe and antistrophe; **'While some said "He is a good man", others said "No, he is leading the people astray" ';** or **'Others said, "This is the Messiah". But some said, "Is the Messiah going to come from Galilee?" '** (7.12; 41: cf. also 8.30; 9.16; 9.45f; 12.11.); like the chorus of Theban Women in *Seven against Thebes* (1072-84), some siding with the herald, others with Antigone.

Hoi Iudaioi

Whereas all the Synoptic gospels make clear that it was the chief priests, the lawyers ('scribes') and the Sanhedrin ('the assembly', 'the elders') who wanted Jesus dead, who condemned him and delivered him to Pilate and then worked on the crowd to make them hostile also, the widespread use in the Fourth Gospel of the term *hoi Iudaioi*, most commonly translated as 'the Jews', for all those who opposed Jesus at Jerusalem, certainly appears to lay the blame for the crucifixion on the whole nation. I shall suggest that that was never the author's intention, but resulted from his choice of the Men of Jerusalem as his chorus.

He would certainly not have written a pro-Jewish gospel; for in the second half of the first century separation and antagonism between traditionalist Jews and those who were called Christians had been steadily growing.[75] The Christian church as a whole had, too, ever since it first admitted non-Jews, moved further and further away from Jewish law and ritual obligation. The Jewish War against Rome, from 65–70 AD, accelerated the split. The Jews of Palestine had shaken the empire, and were regarded as serious enemies to Rome. The Christian Jews of Palestine, avoiding the conflict, must, to the rest of their nation, have seemed disloyal.

In the aftermath, Jews were subject to severe reprisals, while Christians sought to show themselves always loyal to Rome; thus both Luke and Matthew make Jesus before the high priest avoid claiming to be the Messiah, which had revolutionary overtones; and they try to exonerate Pilate from his responsibility for a crucifixion which in fact only he could have ordered; as indeed he would have done, without hesitation. The Christian interpretation of the destruction of the temple and the holy city in the war as God's punishment for that crucifixion, can only have soured relations with the Jews even further. A little before the writing of John the synagogues had decided to exclude all Christians, making the split formal.[76]

The evangelist, therefore, would not have written a pro-Jewish gospel; but neither need he have intended any kind of anti-Semitic racist propaganda. I suggest that *hoi Iudaioi* should, through out this gospel, be translated not as 'the Jews' but as the 'Judaeans', which was its original meaning, although by John's time it was also often used to cover Judaeans, Galileans, and the vast number of expatriate Jews,[77] of whom there were communities in almost every large city abroad: to include the entire nation, in fact. It is this confusion of identities which has done untold damage.

My reason for choosing 'Judaeans' here is that every tragedy must have a chorus, and in the majority of plays the chorus are inhabitants of the city where the play is set: Women of Troy, Women of Trachis, Phoenican Maidens (actually temple slaves at Thebes), Men of Thebes, Men of Argos, Men of Pherae and so on. The natural choice for a tragedy set in Jerusalem would have been the Men of Jerusalem, *hoi Hierosolumitai,* and so the chorus may even have been designated for the play. The single use of that name, in John 7.25, might well be a lone survival, never amended, from the play script which may have been the author's first draft;[78] just one more instance of the author's oversights when putting together his new and old material.

However, since *Hierosolumitai* is a very awkward word for frequent use, after the play became a novel and these people had constantly to be named[79] the author probably felt that *hoi Iudaioi*, the Men of Judaea, sounded better and would be easier for his reader; it was certainly easier for the writer. Yet, in the extended narrative which we have now, *hoi Iudaioi* are still, unmistakably, the Men of Jerusalem. From the start, when they send priests and Levites *from Jerusalem* to question the Baptist (1.19), to the crucifixion, which many of them go out to see '*because it was near the city*', no use of *hoi Iudaioi* requires any other interpretation; and many demand this one.[80] When '**for fear of the Jews**' is mentioned, those to be feared are always those in Jerusalem, nowhere else; '**a feast of the Jews**' means a feast at Jerusalem; and when Jews turn up in Galilee and criticise Jesus' Living Bread speeches, the author seems to be recalling Mark's similarly critical '**scribes from Jerusalem**' (Mk.7.1.) Sometimes the link is explicit: in the Lazarus story, '**Bethany was a mile or two outside Jerusalem, and many of the Jews had come to comfort Martha and Mary**' (*NEB* paraphrases as '**many of the people had come from the city**'); and at 7.25, the one instance of *Hierosolumitai,* these Jerusalemites have previously been termed *Iudaioi,* during the same debate.

At no point can *hoi Iudaioi* in this gospel be properly translated as 'the Jews', which in English refers to the whole race; in John, if the Jewish nation is meant, Caiaphas (11.50) and Pilate (18.35) correctly use *ho ethnos,* the race.[81] The harm done by the misinterpretation has been terrible, and must be deeply regretted; but we may absolve the evangelist of intending to blame the whole race for what was done in Jerusalem. He merely took the Men of Jerusalem, the city where his play was set, for his chorus, in the traditional way, and made them the antagonists in the drama.

What made this such an unfortunate choice was that later, in his novel, he worked up the tension and excitement further by frequent references to their hostility. The recurrent motif of *dia ton phobon tōn Ioudaiōn*, 'for fear of the Judaeans',[82] repeated in those words at 7.13, 19.38, and 20.19, and in different phrasing in 7.1, 9.22, and 11.54, results from the novelist trying to heighten suspense in his novel. It was simply a distortion of history for literary purposes; but, regrettably, no less harmful because of that.

The Flexible Identity of Hoi Iudaioi.

If *hoi Iudaioi,* the Judaeans, in the gospel narrative began as a chorus of Men of Jerusalem in a play, that would solve many problems of identity which scholars have found baffling.

The term is used some 67 times in John, of which we may here ignore 5 which occur in the phrase '**King of the Jews**' and 6 referring to ethnic feasts and practices. The remaining 56, which have no Synoptic precedents, refer to a body of people who play an active part in the story, but whose identity is elusive.[83] At times these Judaeans seem to be equated with the Pharisees. John's Pharisees have a great deal of unhistorical authority in Jerusalem, to the extent even of sending 'officers' to arrest Jesus (7.32; 18.3); there, and also in 11.47, 57, their authority is linked with that of the chief priests, and the Pharisees are distinguished from the Judaeans in 11.46, where '**some of** (the Judaeans) **went to the Pharisees**'. Yet, in the aftermath of the Blind Man's Healing, Pharisees (9.13, 15, 16, 40) and Judaeans (9.18, 22,) seem to be used interchangeably, both parties having authority. (In fact, under Roman rule, civil authority in Jerusalem was at that time vested in the chief priests, who were not Pharisees but a Sadducean clique.[84]) Earlier John has said that it was also the Judaeans who sent priests and Levites to question the Baptist (1.19), but these same envoys were next said to have been sent by the Pharisees (1.24). The Judaeans are distinguished from *ho ochlos* (7.11f), the ordinary people (the same ignorant masses condemned by the Pharisees in 7.49); yet, as shown above, at other times they seem simply to be inhabitants of Jerusalem, with no special rank or function.

Clearly *hoi Iudaioi* exemplify Rehm's '**extremely flexible notion of identity';** and as the Men of Jerusalem, the chorus of a play, their words might be expected to show attitudes varying from one scene to another, and diverse opinions at times from different groups within the chorus. Were I producing such a play today, I would have one half of the chorus dressed as particularly religious Jews, with their prayer-shawls and phylacteries, and the chorus-leader robed as an important priest; the other half dressed contrastingly as humbler folk.[85] It is not known, and may be thought unlikely, that ancient dramatists needed or chose to be so helpful to their audiences; but, whether distinguished by dress or not, the two groups would unite in the great choral hymns, yet often in dialogue disagree with each other. By the end of the trial, however, the whole chorus are united against Jesus; which is not far from the historical fact – provided we always remember that these are the people of Jerusalem, not the nation as a whole.

Problems solved

If scenes designed for a chorus have been transposed into the narrative of a novel, that could account for some other incongruities. After the cured Blind Man has been **'cast out of the synagogue'** by a group variously called Judaeans and Pharisees, there are still Pharisees actually *with* Jesus (*met' autou*) to hear what he says when he meets the outcast again (John 9.40). In narrative, this is implausible because, in John, all 'the Pharisees' are always depicted as hostile to Jesus; and since the man had been expelled from synagogue for championing Jesus against the authorities, the Pharisees would hardly now be associating with either of them. But the chorus of a play is, normally, present in the orchestra throughout the play,[86] able to re-enter or leave the dialogue as the playwright chooses.

Again, the concept of a divided chorus, strophe against antistrophe, solves the puzzle that in 8.31 Jesus addresses **'the Judaeans who had believed in him'**, yet six verses later is saying **'You wish to kill me'**. Barrett (1978, p.346) comments, with restraint, that John is writing very carelessly here or else means that their faith was very deficient. However, if the author has imagined half his chorus applauding what Jesus has said already (**'As he said these things, many believed in him'**, 8.30), it is to them that Jesus says **'If you abide in my word (...) the truth will set you free'**; but then the hostile half of the chorus respond angrily that they, the seed of Abraham, are nobody's slaves, and so attract, first rebuttal (8.34ff), and then his strongest criticism (8.37-47).

Philip Oakeshott

Choral Fragments?

i) The Prologue

The most unusual feature of this gospel is its 'prologue' (John 1.1--18), in which the author sets out his entire plot expressed in terms of a cosmic theology. Such a prologue belongs to drama, and the 'draft play' hypothesis offers a reason why these verses should stand first and be in a semi-poetical mode. The conjectured rewriting into a novel would then explain the later insertion (as many critics have held it to be) of the verses dealing with the Baptist (1.6f, 15); not a crude interpolation by another hand, but a deliberate amplification by the author when, instead of going on to turn his original draft into Greek verse, he changed course and expanded his first draft into a novel.

A prologue, technically, is anything which is spoken, or sung, *before the entry of the chorus*; and the sudden change to first person, **'And the Word became flesh and pitched his tent among us; and we beheld his glory...'** might have been the opening choric line, for choruses often speak in the first person. The great, impersonal declaration of the theology of incarnation would however have already been declaimed by an actor, costumed as an angel or Wisdom, from the top of the skene, the theologeion, 'the place from which the gods speak'.

ii). Jesus to Nicodemus (3.11—21).

This 'speech' begins explicitly as a reply: **'Jesus answered and said to (Nicodemus), "Are you the teacher of Israel and you do not know these things?"** (3.10). In the next sentence, however, comes a change to the first person plural: '**Truly, truly I tell you that we speak what we know and we bear witness to what we have seen, and you people do not accept our witness.**' This 'we' is quite inconsistent with the very central use of 'I' in other speeches by Jesus. Is '**we witness to what we have seen**' to be taken as editorial, the statement of the post-resurrection Christian community (Barrett 1978, p.211f)? Or of the group who testify to the truth of the 'eye-witness' at the end of the gospel? Or is it, perhaps, the characteristically first personal speech-mode of a chorus?

The speech, beyond its opening sentence, does not seem to be meant for Jesus. Rather, as it moves on into the enormous claim made for him, '**God so loved the world that he gave his only son...**', it has reverted to the third person and to the style of the opening. The writer has again produced something which, save for the fact that it is not in verse, is not unlike the deep comments, on the dealings of gods with men, often given to the chorus of a Greek tragedy. So perhaps most of Jesus' speech here was originally intended for a chorus.

iii). The Baptist (3.27-36)

Only a few verses later, following a speech given to the Baptist, '**He must increase and I must decrease**', the writer reverts once more to broader, less personal comment with '**The one who comes down from heaven is above all... Whoever believes in the son has eternal life...**' (3.31--36). This too has affinity with the generalised wide-ranging comment of a chorus.

The treatment of high matters in a poetical way is not, of course, limited to drama. It can be found in Greek and Latin poetry: Simonides speaks movingly of humanity's struggles with fate or fortune, Virgil looks deep into life and death. In the letters of Paul, similar topics are sometimes rendered in an almost lyrical prose, as in his praise of *Agapē* (1. Cor.13). We may note, however, that Plato has put his equally fervent praise of *Eros*, which could make a fine chorus, into the mouth of a dramatist (*Symposium*, 197 C,D,E); for it is only in a play (or perhaps in an epic poem) that one may expect to find such comment on the deeper issues interspersed with the telling of a story.

Yet in spite of their high topics and cosmic viewpoint, these passages, not being in verse, are not finished choruses and probably never were. They suggest, rather, an author writing with a chorus in mind, possibly making a draft which he intended to turn later into an appropriate verse-form.

9

Jesus At Jerusalem:
A Tentative Reconstruction

With now a case made out for the theatrical nature of much of John, it is time to demonstrate that a draft tragedy can easily be disinterred from the text simply by taking a number of scenes set at or near Jerusalem, *in the exact order in which they occur in the narrative*. To do so should show that the thesis advanced in this book is at least feasible.

Opening Scenes

The suggested play, which we may call *Jesus at Jerusalem*, would open, as stated above, with some heavenly being, such as an angel or Wisdom, appearing on the theologeion to declaim that '**In the beginning was the Word**' (John 1.1-5, 10-13). The actual prologue ends at the entry of the chorus, costumed as 'Men of Jerusalem' and singing, '**And the Word became flesh and pitched his tent amongst us...**' (1.14,16-18).

It has been mentioned in Chapter Eight that choruses often sing in halves, putting different points of view; and I have suggested dressing this chorus to differentiate between plainly costumed ordinary folk and highly religious Jews, 'Pharisees', with their prayer shawls and phylacteries, with the leader of the chorus, making up the total of fifteen singers, costumed as a priest. Then, at different times, the choreographer could set the common folk in front of the devout singers, or vice versa, or marshal the choir into two separate groups, taking turns to sing. This would help the fluid and flexible identity of the chorus, while contrasting costumes would enhance the choreography of their dancing movement. There is, indeed, no sure evidence to show that choruses in classical tragedy ever wore differentiated costumes; although some problems would be solved if the chorus in Aeschylus' *Suppliant Maidens* consisted of two halves, eight maidens and seven attendants; or in Euripides' *Suppliant Women*, of six or seven mothers, seven sons and an attendant or two to make up the number. Even when the chorus were fifteen women of Trachis, say, or fifteen Phoenician maidens, it would surely have been natural and artistically sound to clothe them with some variety, of colour if of nothing else.

On this occasion the chorus might have been led in by the common folk, exemplifying here '**those who believed in his name**'; but now the Baptist enters, with two disciples, to confront from the stage the chorus-leader, with attendant 'Levites' and 'Pharisees', below. From the *orchestra* the Priest demands '**Who are you?**' and receives his answers (1.19-27); and as the chorus draw back towards the sides of the *orchestra,* the leading actor, who spoke the prologue, now enters below, and walks across, masked and dressed as Jesus. The Baptist declaims prophetically, '**Look, the Lamb of God...**', ending '**This is the Chosen of God**' (1.29b-34). He points Jesus out to his two disciples, who run down the ramp to catch Jesus. Jesus turns to see what they want, one perhaps asks where he is staying, and all three exit together (1.38f).

The chorus sing verses (now grafted into the prologue, 1.6-8) honouring the Baptist, while he exits; and extras, perhaps four, enter by one ramp onto the stage as 'Traders', with sheep and goats, small tables and a cageful of pigeons. The tall double-doors are flung open from inside by the two disciples, and Jesus makes an entry, brandishing a whip of cords as he descends to knock over a table or two and scatter the traders, who flee with their livestock and props. Challenged from below by the leader of the chorus, Jesus counters '**Destroy this temple and in three days I will rebuild it**'; the whole chorus comment in amazement and disbelief (2.14-20), while Jesus retires upstage. There he is met by Nicodemus (second actor, first seen as the Baptist), whose questions lead Jesus to proclaim himself the Son of Man. The chorus pick this up with '**God so loved the world... The light has come into the world but people loved the darkness better... The one who comes from on high is above all...**' (3.1-21, 31-6).

Power and Glory

Next come healings, to show the power of Jesus. For brevity, from here on only particular points of staging will be high-lighted. An Old Man is carried on stage on a light bed which, once he has been 'healed', he hoists onto his back. As the rejuvenated man comes forward, carrying his load, and is challenged by the chorus for sabbath-breaking, Jesus 'conceals' himself by standing close to the painted 'pillars' of the porch. From there he steps forward later to assert his own superiority to the claims of the Sabbath (5.3-18, 44-7; 7.19-24).

While the chorus wrangle (7.25-31), a Blind Man taps his way on stage (9.1), led by a small boy. The Blind Man's cure at the property basin has been discussed in Chapter Seven; he returns to argue with the 'Pharisees' in the chorus (9.9-12, 30-41); and the scene closes with Jesus, threatened by the mimed picking up of stones to throw at him (8.59), escaping (10.33-4, 37-9) through the central doorway, 'pursued' by the whole chorus, who exit by both parodoi.[87]

Then Mary and Martha take centre stage, the chorus, now all together, re-enter decorously in procession by one parodos, as mourners from Jerusalem, and the sisters and chorus sing the *kommos* (lament) until Jesus enters at the side, with two or three disciples. At '**Take away the stone**' the disciples haul open the central doors, and Lazarus makes his mute entrance. His joyful sisters lead him away, accompanied by Jesus and the disciples and followed by the 'lay' half-chorus, leaving the 'Pharisee' half-chorus to take the centre of the orchestra and ask what they are to do about the alarming popularity achieved by this prophet; until the chorus leader pronounces the superbly ironic verdict on Jesus, that '**it is expedient that one man should die for the people lest the whole nation perish**' (11.46-51). This is interrupted by the processional re-entry of disciples, leading Jesus on a donkey, and escorted by the humbler half of the chorus, singing and flourishing palm-branches. (Hence, in John 12.12-13, the crowd who, contrary to the Synoptic versions, hearing that Jesus is coming, '**go out**' to meet him, with their symbolic emblems.) They lead a serene and impassive

Jesus round the full circuit of the orchestra, hailing him in song (12.13) as the Messiah: '**Hosanna! Blessed is the one who comes in the name of the Lord, the king of Israel.**' As the procession moves round towards the back of the orchestra, the Pharisees have their turn to sing, and they vent their disgust and dismay (12.19): '**Look, the whole world follows him.**') Jesus has meantime dismounted and from the stage now delivers his '**The hour has come for the Son of Man to be glorified**' speech (12.23-36), followed by thunder and a '**voice from heaven**' off-stage; finally closing with '**Put your trust in the light, so that you may be sons of light**' before he exits once more by the central doors (12.36b). Here is the tragic hero, riding high on popular support, openly defying his enemies, before the sudden change of fortune which will bring him down.

Last Supper and Arrest

A time-break is needed, and the chorus might have sung here a third-personal version of what is now 12.44--50, '**He who believes in me...**' As they sing the scene is reset as 'indoors' by rolling out the mobile platform, the ekkyklema, through the central doorway, with stools behind a small table bearing the plates and wine-cups of a finished meal.[88] Jesus, with two actors as Peter and Thomas enter and take their seats, with an extra or possibly two sitting behind them. The writer has created an active Last Supper scene, both to keep his play moving and, probably, to avoid actual eating on stage, which belongs better to comedy. Jesus gets up, disrobes, takes bowl and sponge from the rear of the platform, and, girded with a towel, washes his disciples' feet (13.4-10,

12-17), despite argument from the second actor as 'Peter'. Reclothed, Jesus makes a farewell speech (13.31-5; 14.1-6, 18-21, 27-31) including an interchange with 'Thomas' (third actor). On the words '**Get up, let us leave this place**', they stand; 'Thomas' and perhaps one extra vanish backstage inconspicuously for a quick change, while Jesus leads Peter and an extra off the ekkyklema (which is then withdrawn) and slowly across to one side of the stage.

There is no need for cinematic realism; Jesus' words make clear that they are leaving, their actions show that they have left, and the withdrawal of the furnished platform cancels the indoor reference; while the actors' slow movement across stage suggests the passing of time.

The new location does not need to be defined:[89] Jesus has time only for a short prayer (17.1-5) before the arrest party (four extras as soldiers, all armed and helmeted, with a slave carrying a lantern or a torch) (18.3) enter below and mount the farther ramp. Jesus advances to centre-stage, asking whom they seek, their leader (possibly the third actor but probably only an extra who could speak a line) says '**Jesus of Nazareth**'. Jesus responds with a resounding '**I AM**' (18.11), and the whole party recoil and fall on their faces. Jesus repeats his question, the leader quavers '**Jesus of Nazareth**', and Jesus confirms his identity. Soldiers and slave get to their feet, but as they approach hesitantly, Peter pushes forward and slashes with a property sword at the slave, who claps both hands, and a capsule of blood, to the side of his head. The author has resisted Luke's suggestion of healing the ear because such a demonstration of miraculous power by Jesus would distract from the *peripateia*; rather, he has Jesus' hands tied at once, to emphasize his fall. The writer's concern is to show Jesus unmoved in misfortune, rejecting violence, and surrendering of his own will to men whom he could have frightened away. Peter, rebuked, at once follows the other disciple, who has exited already (18.8), and Jesus is led down the ramp and into the orchestra. The whole scene has been rife with unsoldierly behaviour, but it makes good theatre.

The soldiers take Jesus, bound, to face the 'High Priest', leader of the chorus (18.24), and then follows the short dialogue (now 18.19-23), with what is now the Levite's line perhaps spoken by the soldiers' leader. The blow he gives would be a sufficient cue for Jesus' dignified remonstrance, but, as suggested in Chapter Seven, a line is needed to identify the chorus leader as the *High* Priest, so that the audience may easily follow what is happening.

Trial and Execution

As the chorus, in words we do not have, condemn Jesus for hubris or lament his fall, he is escorted round the orchestra and up onto the stage again at its other end. The party proceed to the central doorway, where two of the soldiers open the central doors and remain on guard at either side, while the others take Jesus inside. The sentries serve to indicate that the *skene* is now the Praetorium, the governor's Residency. The other two soldiers bring out the seat of judgement (an armed-chair mounted on a small plinth, or a tall chair with a footstool),[90] set it centre-stage and take up positions beside it; and then Pilate makes his entrance, advancing to greet the chorus leader.

After the first exchange with the accusers, Pilate seats himself in his chair and has Jesus brought out (18.33) and stood to one side of it. When that first questioning (18.33-38a) ends with '**What is truth?**', Jesus is taken inside while Pilate goes forward to suggest that Jesus be released as the Passover prisoner (18.38b-40). Thwarted again, Pilate has Jesus brought back, now stripped to the waist and covered in blood, grotesquely crowned with thorn and partially draped with a crimson robe.

Pilate's presentation of this pitiable figure to the chorus leads to chants of '**Crucify**!' and finally to the statement that Jesus made himself out to be the Son of God (19.7), which sends a startled governor hurrying back to question his prisoner once more. As it now reads, although there has been no mention of Jesus being taken inside again, Pilate has to re-enter the Residency to find him (19.9). On stage, Pilate would find his prisoner still standing between his guards further back on the stage and would question him further there; not from the chair, in view of what follows.

In the final round, the governor's declared intention to release Jesus has been checkmated by the threat to denounce him, Pilate, as disloyal to the emperor. '**Then he led Jesus out** (*on stage, he leads him forward*) **and sat him in the chair of justice**' and appealed for clemency: '**Behold your king... Shall I crucify your king?**' Historically implausible in the highest degree, but visually effective and good dramatic irony.

When finally the chorus are brought to cry '**We have no king but Caesar**', Pilate orders the soldiers (this seems the proper meaning of '**he handed him over to** *them* **to be crucified**') to take Jesus away for execution. Two soldiers lead Jesus out through the doorway, Pilate follows, the other two then remove the chair and close the doors behind them.

While the chorus sing (perhaps strophe and antistrophe, one group stressing the blasphemer's guilt while the other grieves for the death of the healer) a procession enters by the *parodos*: '**and carrying his cross himself,** (i.e., tied and 'nailed' to the cross-beam) '**he went out to what is called the Place of the Skull**' (19.17), a lone, tragic figure, escorted only by the four soldiers specified later (19.23).

When the chorus began, the ekkyklema, fitted with a socketed upright, would have been rolled out ready, so that Jesus, led on through the side entrance below stage, could toil first up the ramp and then up again to the top of the ekkyklema, where he is 'crucified', standing on its top. Then the four soldiers sit around and dice for the clothes (19.23), while Jesus' mother and the favourite disciple, (but not the other two Maries of 19.25, who would merely clutter the stage) come up the ramp to the stage and stand to either side of the ekkyklema, so that the lonely victim remains high above seated soldiers and standing friends.

The chorus have been still singing their lament against the visual background of a crucifixion tableau; when they fall silent, unquantified time has elapsed. The writer has cut out Mark's jeering crowd, and there follows the tender passage in which the mother of Jesus is consigned to the care of the Beloved Disciple, who takes her away with him (19.27). Then Jesus calls out that he is thirsty and is given a wine-soaked sponge by one of the soldiers. He calls out again, that his task is accomplished, and 'dies'. A spear with a retractable blade may have been used for the thrust which confirms to the audience that the hero is truly dead.

Death on the stage was common enough for Aristotle to list it amongst theatrical 'calamities'. Possibly the author weighed the alternative of using a 'messenger', a soldier reporting to Pilate or a spectator to the chorus, to describe the crucifixion; but sensibly chose the visual effect of the execution and the emotional appeal of the Mother and Friend scene. On an open stage, however, a corpse is always a problem, solved here by the use of the ekkyklema.

To clear the stage is fast and easy, with the ekkyklema simply withdrawn, taking Jesus, still on his cross, with the soldiers following it; but there must also be a sense of time passing before the audience can be ready for the final scenes; and it is clear that the Burial which follows (19.38-42), having no dialogue and one wholly new character (Joseph of Arimathea) appearing from nowhere, could never have formed part of a play. The chorus here could both close the execution scene and then proceed to inform the audience that Jesus had been buried and that now (no need to specify day or time) Mary, whose brother he once brought back to life, is on her way to visit Jesus' tomb and do what she may to honour his name and assuage her own grief.

The Hero's Triumph

Thus, when Mary Magdalene enters, the scene has been set for her, and the audience know that the central doorway is now the tomb which she is approaching. (If the chorus have not covered this, Mary herself can tell it in monologue.) Mary would now speak movingly of how she hopes to honour the Master they had all loved. By now she is weeping but, noticing that one of the central doors is half-open, she goes to pull it wide, and then opens the other, revealing two figures in shiny white robes (one is the third actor) sitting at either end of a bare shelf.

After their brief interchange, Mary turns away and meets Jesus, and during their emotional dialogue (20.11-17), while all eyes are on them, the angels quietly pull the doors shut. Jesus and Mary exit to opposite sides. There would then have to be a chorus long enough to allow Jesus to change into a shining robe, while the angel-actor sheds one, and both take places on the ekkyklema, with table and stools and two or three extras. These, with the third actor now as Thomas again, are seated; Jesus, covered by a dark cloth or cloak, is invisible, crouched behind the covered table.

The platform is rolled out, then Mary enters excitedly from the side, to tell the disciples that she has seen the Lord (20.18). Thomas comes down stage to dispute this with her, and while everyone is watching them, with Thomas passionately declaring that he will not believe this unless he can see the marks of the nails, Jesus suddenly springs up, in his shining robe. At the same instant, or better a fraction earlier, the seated disciples leap to their feet, obscuring his upward movement, and immediately step back and away in wonder, to reveal, alone on the platform, a figure in shining robes, arms outstretched to show the nail-marks and confound the doubter. Thomas' ringing declaration, '**My Lord and my God!**' is followed by Jesus' closing line (20.29), epitomising the author's emphasis on belief as the indispensable virtue. Then the ekkyklema is withdrawn, carrying Jesus in a posture of blessing and followed off by all the disciples. The chorus would cover their going with a few lines to end the play; a *reprise* of some of 3.16-21 might serve.

This is, I repeat, a feasibility study only. It does not prove that there ever was such a play, nor, if there was, that my reconstruction is necessarily correct. What it does show is that it is not unrealistic to say that the author of John *might* have begun by drafting a play, dealing with Passion Week only; most of which can be found, spread throughout the gospel but still largely in its original sequence.

If he did, there is a definite impression that, for one of many possible reasons, he gave up writing his play before he had completely finished the draft version, since not only is there no trace of verse, but nor is there anything to suggest many of the choruses that it would have required. Perhaps he had already realised that his poetic skills did not run to turning his work from prose into good Greek verse. Perhaps it was pointed out to him that he still had too many characters, so that his actors would each have too many small parts to play; or perhaps, that he would never find a sponsor willing to put on a play about Jesus, with so much anti-Christian feeling about. He might even have found the elders of his church condemning the idea of having anything to do with that sink of iniquity, the theatre. For whatever reason, he chose to turn his draft into the basis of a Greek novel.

10

The Value Of John: A Personal View.

John as Historical Fiction.

To sum up the case for John as a work of sincere and inspired fiction: it was shown that the Fourth Gospel, as it now exists, has the form of a historical novel, with the evangelist employing all the skills of a novelist. (Ancient Greek novels differ from modern ones, although hardly more than those of the nineteenth century from those of today; but while styles and topics change, the writer's skills remain essentially the same.)

Virtually all scholars agree, however, that the finished gospel was not written as a single whole, but must be the product of some process of revision, edition, conflation or rewriting. For that there is abundant evidence; but as to the nature of the process, or the nature of the original document, agreement is still to seek. So, secondly, I have suggested that the process consisted of rewriting a drafted play to turn it into a novel.

Examination of the many theatrical elements in John can certainly suggest that the Fourth Evangelist's first intention was for a tragedy: not merely in the sense that the narrative we now have conforms to a notional 'tragic pattern', although that is, to some degree, true; nor in the sense that his work consists of two 'acts', or five 'acts'; nor yet that one or two episodes can be compared to a dramatist's use of an 'inner and outer stage', as C.H. Dodd and others have proposed. It is theatrical in the literal sense that the author created a complete plot, worked out each scene and drafted at least some of his choruses; although he stopped before turning his prose into the verse which was the indispensable vehicle for Greek tragedy. The reconstruction in Chapter Nine has shown that this is a genuine possibility; a series of scenes which could make a complete play designed for the Greek stage actually does exist within the Gospel of John.

Furthermore, a number of episodes imitate or echo scenes from surviving Greek tragedies; some seem to be designed for visual effectiveness in a theatre, some betray other aspects of stagecraft, and some suggest the limitations of the three-actor cast. Again, dramatic necessity, stagecraft and the presence of a chorus would account for numerous perplexities and deviations from the Synoptic tradition; while a great many apparent inconsistencies and jumps in the narrative could result from the reworking and expansion of the script of a play to make a novel.

Why the author should have abandoned his draft and then transposed it into a novel is something we cannot know; but clearly he decided at some point that a novel was the preferable medium. A strong probability must be that he felt that he could better satisfy his creative urge by releasing his story from the constraints of theatre and using a broader canvas. Nor should we suppose him immune from the wish to see his work reach a wider public than was likely for a tragedy which relatively few would read and no sponsor was likely to put on. Since he was an evangelist setting forth his own concept of Jesus and his work, death and resurrection, and hoping -- with the guidance of the Spirit, as may be inferred from his Last Supper Discourses -- to strengthen, comfort and counsel all fellow-disciples, then the wider his readership the better.

It would, however, be a serious mistake to suppose that because he turned to narrative, he therefore ceased to be a creative writer and became a historian. Nothing, I suggest, could be farther from the truth. There has been a great reluctance amongst scholars to concede a genuine, rather than a purely nominal, creativity to the Fourth Evangelist; but a truly creative instinct must create, it will not be satisfied merely to reproduce. John, as Clement of Alexandria said, '**composed a spiritual gospel**'; it would be hard to contradict him even if he had said 'a spiritual masterpiece'.

The Son of God

As he makes extremely clear in his prologue, John holds that Jesus is divine, and appears on earth as God made flesh, showing us what the invisible God is like. Now Acts had spoken of '**a man attested to you by acts of power and miracles and signs which God did through him**', who had then, having been '**raised up**' from the tomb and exalted at the right hand of God, been made '**both Lord and Messiah**'; Paul, although he had received firsthand accounts from Peter and from James the Lord's brother, himself thought of a supernaturally pre-existent Christ[91] who '**emptied himself**' of his supernatural attributes (Phil.2.6-8). The fourth evangelist, however, sees Jesus not only as unquestionably divine but as retaining divine powers on earth; resembling in this such pagan gods as, for example, Dionysus in *The Bacchae*.

On the other hand, the great stress laid in the Prologue on the Word becoming flesh, and the corresponding emphasis in Chapters 20 and 21 on his resurrected body as genuine and substantial, show that John will have no truck with the Docetic claims that the human body of Jesus was without substance, an '**appearance (*dokē*)**' which only seemed to suffer on the cross. His incarnate God is not beyond human grief, as when he weeps at the tomb of Lazarus, nor invulnerable to physical wounds and death. The Lamb of God goes to the sacrifice, not under human duress but of his own choice; but the crucifixion is human agony, the pain and the humanity made plain as the dying man struggles courageously to make suitable provision for his mother.

Yet, throughout, John is principally concerned to proclaim the divinity of Jesus. His vital point is that men must accept the supernatural nature of Jesus, the belief that he is the Christ, the Son of God, so that by believing this they may partake in the imperishable life which he alone can give them. So, in healings, whether in Galilee or Jerusalem, John presents cures unprecedented in human experience; in the addresses to crowds, he presents uncompromisingly a Jesus claiming direct divine authority, overriding the Law or human judgement, making himself, as the evangelist points out, the same as God, *ison tou theou* (5.18). He will come to judge the dead, not as Daniel's Son of Man, which seems to have been how Peter saw him, but as Son of God, and that, in a sense no Jew would ever have accepted. '**I and the Father are one**', he claims (10.30).

John deals in metaphor rather than parable, and Jesus proclaims himself to be The Living Bread: '**if any one eats this bread, he will live for ever**', and '**Whoever eats my flesh and drinks my blood abides in me and I in him**'; the Good Shepherd, the True Vine, the Way, the Truth and the Life: '**no one comes to the Father, except through me**' (14.6).

For those who feel today that, in John, Jesus claims to know too much, and seems at times to be preaching a rather exclusive Christianity, Mark's picture of Jesus may seem nearer to the facts. Yet even so, '**he came to his own folk and his own folk would not receive him**' is precisely Mark's story of the Passion; and John's claim that, while no one has ever seen God, Jesus has shown us what God is like (1.18), seems to be entirely justified – particularly when we are reading Mark.

Creative Writing

As dramatist John has given us such great scenes as the Expulsion of the Traders from the Temple, the Raising of Lazarus, the Trial before Pilate, The Crucifixion, and the two Resurrection scenes with Mary Magdalene and with Thomas – scenes which are all the better because most of them owe something to Sophocles.

As novelist, John created such stories as for example, the Wedding at Cana, the Samaritan Woman at the Well,

Washing the Disciples' Feet, and that Breakfast by the Lake which forms the epilogue to his novel. These we should accept as excellent fiction, told clearly and not without humour, as vehicles for his personal insights into the power of the Logos, the right way to worship, the secret of leadership or the resurrection experience. It is a waste of time to seek for hypothetical traditions or community disputes to explain scenes which need no explanation; for nothing is more satisfying to an author than the imaginary scene which he or she has contrived from nothing.

Some memorable episodes have indeed been created in rewriting dramatic scenes for the novel. One such is the healing of the Man Born Blind, in which the actual healing was, I have suggested, very clearly designed for staging, whereas the subsequent dispute, in which John gives his dry sense of humour full rein, must, for the most part, have been developed later, in the novel. But how far can such a work, novel or drama, contribute to our knowledge and understanding of Jesus?

John and History

It was once suggested to me that it is pointless today to argue that John is fiction, because '**Everyone knows that John is not history**'; and, up to a point, that is true. Few, if any, scholars would today claim John as an accurate account of the ministry of Jesus; nonetheless, many will invoke particular statements from John in support of, or even as the ground for, their arguments.

In Michael Grant's historical study, *Jesus*, for example, there are sixty-two Fourth Gospel references, of which approximately one third are correctly rejected as late or fanciful, another third deployed in support of the Synoptics, but the remaining third used as sole ground for a particular assertion. The perhaps less objective, but very radical, Jesus Seminar claims, as important to our understanding of the Kingdom of Heaven in the Synoptics, that some of Jesus' disciples had formerly followed the Baptist (Funk 1996, pp.3f.), an assertion for which there is no evidence at all except John 1.35-42,[92] a statement from a source which the seminar do not usually seem to trust. Even a more conservative scholar like James Dunn, in his well argued study of Mark's 'Messianic Secret' (in Tuckett, p.123), weakens his case a little by using John 6.15 to show that the Feeding of the Crowd in Mark 6.35-44 had, and was recognised as having, messianic significance; for there is nothing in Mark's account to suggest this, and what John said later is not, I suggest, valid evidence for what Mark himself meant. Far from being discounted as a historical source, John is frequently invoked whenever it offers support for a writer's theory.

No statement in John, I suggest, ought to be considered historically valid unless confirmed by Mark or by reliable outside evidence. John's date for the crucifixion, for example, is corroborated by a later Bishop of Ephesus, speaking for the whole church of 'Asia' (Western Turkey) -- where, if tradition is correct, this gospel was written – and also by the Talmud (see *Appendix C*); therefore it can be considered reliable. But that is an isolated case: we may, for example, accept that John is correct in having Jesus tried and condemned by Pilate, on which all the Synoptics agree, and which Tacitus confirms; but not so in his details of trial and crucifixion, in which even the now traditional nails in the hands are no more than an inference from John 21.25b, with no corroboration anywhere else at all.

This yardstick of independent confirmation will allow a sounder and less confused picture of the many events which in John have been recast to suit the author's artistic intent. If we are realistic, above all about the non-existence of that Beloved Disciple whom so many scholars still strive to preserve and identify, our understanding of what Jesus really did and said becomes clearer and less distorted; while John becomes more, not less, inspiring when we no longer need to try to reconcile its stories with history.

Sacrament and Spirit

Nonetheless this Fourth Gospel has something to offer to the church historian through what it tells us about the practice and theology of the turn-of-first-century Christians. John emphasizes Jesus as the authority for the church's sacraments. He claims that Jesus, if not actually himself baptizing, certainly authorized his disciples to baptize, and he has Jesus telling Nicodemus that one must be born again 'of water and the spirit'. His story is true, not to the life of Jesus, but to the belief and practice of the church to which the author belonged.

It is therefore, on the face of it, surprising that this gospel does not relate the sharing of the bread and wine at the Last Supper. There was, however, no need to establish that the sacrament of Communion was instituted by Jesus himself, since St. Paul and the three Synoptic evangelists had set this beyond doubt. Further, if my basic thesis is accepted, there would have been no room in the original drama for a specific Supper scene as well as a Footwashing; to maintain the pace of the play the meal must already be presumed concluded before the Footwashing scene opens, so that the action moves on quickly to the Arrest. Later, when the author rewrote his work, he was more concerned to expand his discourses on the last commandment and the promise of the Spirit. What he did do, as he added in a Galilean ministry, was to emphasize the element of miraculous power, which he saw in the Communion, through two of the miracles which he attributed to Jesus. In the Feeding in the Wilderness the bread is, according to John, without question multiplied by miracle [6.14, 51], which is followed up by the claim that '**he who eats my flesh and drinks my blood lives in me, and I in him…. The one who eats this bread will live for ever**' (6.56,58); and earlier, at Cana, water was transformed into a very special wine. Together these suggest that the rite of sharing the bread and wine is seen by John not simply as a symbolic commitment to remember and to share in the sacrificial role of Jesus, but as having in itself some miraculous power of grace.

This may suggest that the church was beginning to think in terms parallel to those of such mystery cults as the Eleusinian mysteries, Mithraism, the Orphics and the Dionysiacs of the Gentile world. Christians too now had their initiation ceremony, their sacred ritual feast, and eternal life guaranteed to the faithful initiate. But 'parallel to' need not mean 'derived from': if the mystery sects had any influence here it was probably that their concepts seemed to confirm those the church was developing in its own practice. The author is probably giving the viewpoint of the church where he worshipped; and for him and them the essential behind the sacraments was to trust loyally to

Jesus -- **'I am the way; no one comes to the Father save through me.' 'He who hears my word and trusts in him who sent me has eternal life'** – to follow his example of humility, shown by his washing of their feet, and to be loving: **'love one another, just as I have loved you'**.

In John the sacraments themselves are absolutely essential – **unless you eat the flesh of the Son of man and drink his blood, you have no life in you** (6.53) – but to rely on and listen to the Spirit is also seen by the author as essential for those who would follow the Way: **'The Spirit of truth ... will guide you into all truth'**.

John also says that **'God is spirit, and they that worship him must worship in spirit and in truth'**, which may suggest that the author's church was still distinguished by such worship as Paul describes (1 Cor.14.26-33), with people 'prophesying', or possibly 'speaking in tongues', as they felt prompted by the spirit. (Later the Montanists possibly, and the Quakers certainly, were encouraged in their own special ways of worship by this verse.)

The verse might mean only that no worship, nor 'prophecy', nor sacrament has value unless the worshipper is sincere and humble. However, in Chapter Six John's narrative depicts the words about the absolute need to eat the flesh and to drink the blood as being a stumbling-block for many of Jesus' disciples; which may mean that this had been a point of dissension between members of John's own church. If so, his emphasis on the spirit as equally essential – **It is the spirit that gives life; the flesh is worth nothing** (6.63) – might suggest that the evangelist was trying here to reconcile such differences.

Memorable Sayings

Any work of art is open to different interpretations, and the greater the work the more will be the different ways of looking at it. One of our author's great strengths was the ability to encapsulate an important insight in memorable words. There are the great assertions: **'I am the Bread of Life', 'I am the Good Shepherd', 'I am the Way, the Truth and the Life', 'God is spirit, and those who worship him must worship in spirit and in truth', 'If mine were an earthly kingdom, then my followers would fight.'** There are the promises: **'In my Father's house there are many lodgings', 'You are my friends, if you keep my commandments', 'Peace I leave with you; I give you *my* peace, not as the world gives', 'Do not let your hearts be troubled'.** And the great commandment: **'Just as I have loved you, so you must love each other. By this everyone will recognise you as my disciples.'**

There are others which I have quoted earlier and more, perhaps, which I have not; but everyone will find their own treasures.

The human Jesus

In his Prologue the author has stated uncompromisingly that the divine[93] Creative Power of God became incarnate, was made flesh, and **'pitched his tent amongst us'**. In the many controversies Jesus seems, in what we have suggested was his theatrical *persona*, to be provocatively confrontational, sure of his own divine wisdom, concerned to defeat all the arguments of his opponents, leaving to them no answers but anger and violence. Yet in what I shall call sketches -- the short scenes, mostly written for the novel, which could be termed 'reminiscences' if they were not pure invention – the author shows a warmer, more tender Jesus, kindly and friendly, for whom it would be natural, as a final bequest, to command his disciples to love each other, and to call them his friends (John 13.34; 15.14f.); and, because John was such a talented writer, he has made these scenes very graphic and so, truly memorable.

In the Wedding at Cana Jesus not only reveals his divine nature by the astounding miracle he works, but does this in the context of saving his hosts at a country wedding from great embarrassment; and we are invited to enjoy the astonishment of the master of ceremonies as he savours the quality of the wine made, although he does not know it, from water. With the Woman of Samaria Jesus shows himself friendly, to her surprise, and tolerant. The humour, which starts with her asking for the Living Water to save herself the daily trudge to the well, is taken further when she goes home and describes Jesus, who has used divine omniscience to remind her gently that she is no better than she should be, as having told her '**everything that I ever did**'. Later, her neighbours snub her by saying that now, having heard Jesus themselves, they do believe, but not because of anything *she* might have said; which may at one level be a reminder that the truth about Jesus relies on eye-witness, not on hearsay, but is also a neat little cameo of our human tendency to put each other down.

The Miracle of the Loaves and Fishes, although not greatly changed from Mark, is delightfully enhanced with the little boy who offers his own food, and also given a dramatic escape scene when the crowd afterwards wish to make Jesus a king. The controversy which follows the healing of the Man Born Blind is human and even humorous in the evasion offered by the man's parents and by his own sturdy common sense replies (John 9.20, 30-3). The Raising of Lazarus, already vivid and graphic in the original play-script, has now the preliminary discussion with the disciples, who misunderstand Jesus, and Thomas' pessimistic loyalty -- a section which has been noted as not advancing the story, but which does reveal the disciples as all too human themselves.

At the Last Supper, Washing the Disciple's Feet is not only a concrete demonstration of the dictum in Mark, it also displays Peter's customary impulsiveness and Jesus' firm and kindly handling of his over-enthusiasm. Next comes the tense scene of the identification, made only to the favourite disciple and Peter, of the traitor; concluded memorably with Judas symbolically departing into outer darkness – '**Once he had taken that morsel, he went out immediately. And it was night**'. Then Jesus prepares the remaining eleven to manage without himself, and the chapters of reiterated teaching are enlivened with moments of further impulsiveness from Peter, naivety (from Philip), enquiry (from Jude) and doubt (from Thomas), as well as the puzzlement of the whole band. All of these human foibles are patiently dealt with.

The Tragic Hero

Now the author reverts to the Jesus of theatre. Gethsemane is specified in the narrative only as '**a garden**' or '**orchard**', for in a play it would simply have been an undefined location, nowhere in particular. Here Jesus is not the tormented human of Mark 14.32-42, but serenely heroic, showing himself to have the power to frighten off the soldiers, but instead, sacrificing himself in accordance with God's plan – which here Jesus fully understands -- yet ensuring the safety of his followers. He is humane, but resembles the superior, 'godlike' man, unmoved by human fears and emotions, who was the ideal of the Stoics.

Throughout his trial Jesus continues in this noble role, not a silent victim as in Mark but fluently propounding a version of his messianic role as a heavenly king. Whether or not Jesus had ever believed himself to be the nation's Messiah, certainly it was the concept of the Messiah as the Heavenly Judge who would come to judge and rule the world, as set out by Peter at Pentecost according to Acts 2.31, 36, which had enabled the disciples after Easter to reconcile their belief in Jesus as God's prophet with his shameful death. But after the Jewish revolt (65-70 AD) an interpretation of heavenly kingship not involving earthly rule would have become important, to distinguish pacifist Christians from rebellious Jews. Also, the hope of an ideal human life on earth, under the rule of God, after an imminent Second Coming of Christ, which is clearly the expectation of St. Paul and the Synoptics, now seemed less immediate, and its proclamation politically inexpedient. So their hope had begun to alter, with human life on an ideal earth being transformed into a heavenly life after death.

In John 18.36, moreover, the evangelist also re-emphasizes the peaceful, harmless attitude which Jesus had indeed commanded (Matt.5.39; Luke 6.29); which is specific (Matt. 26.52; Luke 22.51, John 18.11) at the arrest at Gethsemane; and which the church was still, in that early period, obeying: '*If* **my kingdom belonged to this world, then my servants would fight**.' And it is at the crucifixion that the tender side of Jesus is shown at its costliest, as the tortured man labours to make loving provision for his mother.

The two key resurrection scenes, those with Mary Magdalene and with Thomas (the only ones which our imagined play would have included) are among the author's finest achievements. More perhaps than anything in any other gospel they convey in fiction the experience as it must have been in fact, the vision creating a moment of sudden, total certainty, forever unshakeable. '**My Master!**' says Mary; '**My Lord and my God!**' says Thomas. It is not clear whether the writer means that either touches Jesus (stagecraft suggests that Mary does but Thomas does not) but both are as completely convinced as if they had. Although both scenes are excellent 'theatre', they surely portray very closely how that dramatic experience must have seemed to those who experienced it. What exactly took place on those occasions may be explained or understood in many ways; but to those who were there, this was probably how it felt.

Closure

The last appearance, beside the Lake of Galilee, is well designed and well written as a fitting epilogue to conclude the gospel as a novel. Very properly, therefore, it introduces nothing new to the main plot, but allows the reader to savour at leisure the overwhelming joy of the disciples who now know that their Master is more truly alive than ever. It ties up two loose ends, reconciling Peter with Jesus (or rather, it may be, with himself) and strongly implying that the long-lived John of Ephesus was the witness whom this gospel has repeatedly invoked; perhaps hinting too that he is the same person as John bar Zebedee. It does not matter that there is probably only a faint shadow of truth behind the first claim, and none at all in the second; our creative author has given his book a splendid conclusion.

Themes

The Lamb of God

John's Jesus has been a stumbling block for many because he teaches mostly about himself and his own importance – **'I and my father are one'** -- in long wrangles with, usually, 'the Pharisees'. Again, this divine Jesus must be a man of miracle; so all John's miracles are bigger and better than the Synoptic ones. But much more importantly, **'he came unto his own people, and his own accepted him not'**; Mark had shown Jesus as the innocent sacrifice, whose blood is given **'as a ransom for many'**. John echoes this with Jesus as the Lamb of God.

The innocent sacrifice made to the gods was a favourite theme in drama, and a recurrent motif in the Old Testament.[94] Already the church had begun to think of Jesus as Isaiah's Suffering Servant, the expiatory sacrifice (Mt.8.17), whose submission to his fate is likened to a lamb, going dumbly to the slaughter (Acts 8.32-35). So too, John's Jesus at Gethsemane, accepting that for him God's time has come, is cast in the same mould. Although himself clearly able to control the event, he voluntarily surrenders to the demoralized soldiers and is bound and led away to eventual death. And John, whose church held that Jesus was crucified on the same day that the Passover lambs were slaughtered and their blood offered at the temple altar (see *App.C*), has underlined this by moving Mark's nine o'clock crucifixion to noon, so that it shall coincide more exactly with the sacrifice of the lambs that afternoon.

Not so many people today can accept the idea that an innocent sacrifice could ever be the will of God, but in the ancient world this was the common currency of religion, and very strong in Judaism. It offered not only a possible way of influencing the unseen powers, but a way of understanding our common experience that the least guilty are often those penalized by the greed, anger or thoughtlessness of others, and that those who set the best examples are likely to die for it. John thought as his world and his church thought; moreover, the innocent hero going calmly to death makes great theatre.

Life

John uses *psychē* for the physical life, which we must all lose someday; but mostly in John life is *zōē*, which he uses for the life of God, the essence of the divine, the imperishable life which Jesus embodies and all those who accept Jesus are given. **'The Word was divine... in him was life, and the life was the light of men', 'I am come so that they may have life, and have much more of it.'** (10.10). It is the life which can never be lost, the guarantee of an afterlife, for **'I am the resurrection and the life.'** But the life was also **'the light of men'**.

Light

The Word of God, the expression of God's nature and God's will to humans, is the Light which shines in the darkness of the sinful world. John does not accept the Gnostic dualism by which all our material nature is inherently evil, a prison from which we must escape; on the contrary, every thing in the world was made by the Word of God. Yet he has his own dualism, of light and darkness, found in all creation but most pertinently in the hearts of men. As Nicodemus and the audience are told, '**God sent the Son... not to condemn the world, but that the world should be saved through him.**' And with hindsight John can say '**This is the judgement, that the light came into the world, and men preferred the darkness to the light.**' Unlike the Gnostics, John does not suggest the need for any special or esoteric knowledge (*gnosis*), but, as Jesus himself had taught, only for the willingness to accept the plain, but perhaps to many inconvenient, truth.

The Authorised Version's translation of John 1.9, '**the true light that enlighteneth every man that cometh into the world**' would certainly have encouraged George Fox in his belief that there was '**that of God in everyone**'; and the essence of this belief is not altered by the translation if we must now render it as '**the light that enlightens every human was coming into the world**'. There have been, and are, many people who, regardless of any question of their or anybody's sect or faith, have acted on the assumption that there is something in anyone which can respond to being approached in love and friendship, and have found that this something is often accessible even when not at first apparent. In the terminology of early Quakers, God plants the Seed in everyone; but it must be encouraged to germinate and grow. People must '**turn to the Light**'. John might well agree with the Quakers on this, but his concern is to point to the many people in his narrative whose own mindset made them shut their eyes against the Light and turn away.

Yet the true Light shines out for everyone in this gospel, whether they will accept it or not. In John's teaching the Light and the Spirit seem often to have the same function; the distinction is that the Light is the divine truth as seen in Jesus himself, the Spirit is the guide to truth who came to the early church when the incarnate Light, the human Jesus, was no longer present.

Spirit

Above all, in the discourses at the Last Supper, we have the spirit as known in the experience of the apostles and the earliest church. The spirit is the *paraklētos*, the Counsellor, the Friend in Need, the Guide and Strengthener; he will stay with us forever; and he will lead us to all truth. Again and again John returns to this theme, so it was still important in his time. He speaks as a member of the church, perhaps at Ephesus; '**God is spirit, and those who worship him must worship him in spirit and in truth**'. The promise to the disciples at the Last Supper that the Spirit, the Counsellor, will come only when Jesus himself is gone, is truly a prophecy *ex eventu*: the author foretells the coming of the Spirit because he knows that that had indeed happened.[95] Speaking as prompted by the spirit was the common experience of the early church, not only at Pentecost but recorded over and over in Acts. From St. Paul, who speaks not merely of 'speaking in tongues' but of the intelligible and much more helpful 'prophecy' -- usually known to Quakers as 'ministry' -- we know that it was also a common occurrence in early Christian worship. ('Prophecy' is simply speaking out in the name of God; it may or may not involve foretelling the future.) When teaching Nicodemus, Jesus also links the spirit to baptism; because, as again we may see in Acts, it was also the experience of the first Christians that baptism often led to this manifest sign of the spirit -- speech which, whether intelligible or not, came from deep in the heart and without conscious control.

Love

Love, above all, is the essential quality of God: '**God so loved the world that he gave his only son, in order that whoever puts their trust in him may not perish but have eternal life**' (3.16). It follows that we too must love, and to this theme John repeatedly returns in his Last Supper discourses. '**I am giving you a new commandment, to love each other. By this all men will know that you are my followers, if you have love one for another.**' This emphasis on disciples loving each other may seem limited, but is really crucial: for if we do not love those nearest to us, we shall certainly not truly love anyone else. Moreover, those nearest may often, simply because one is so closely linked to them, be difficult to love; as a modern Quaker has said, '**part of the cost of discipleship is living with the other disciples.**'[96]

As so often in John, Jesus dramatically exemplifies what he teaches. '**No man has greater love than this, that he gives his life for his friend**'; and in the garden, Jesus tells the arrest-squad, '**If you are looking for me, let**

these men go.' Then he goes to give his life, for them and for all the world; but, says John, he also leaves for them his peace; **'my sort of peace I give you, not the sort the world would give you':** not peace as commonly understood, but peace that will last through every calamity or hardship (14.27).

Friendship

There are two Greek verbs which the Authorised Version and many later ones translate indifferently as 'love': *agapaō*, implying the deepest and strongest devotion, and *phileō*, meaning a strong liking or friendship. The difference may be seen in the last chapter of the gospel: when Jesus is asking Peter gradually for less and less, it is the change down from *agapas me*, 'Do you love me?' to *phileis me,* 'Are you my friend?', which makes Peter angry.

But friendship has its own importance. *Phileō* is the word used for Jesus' friendship for Lazarus, and used interchangeably with *agapaō* of his affection for the anonymous 'beloved' disciple –we might say, 'his best friend'. Further, Jesus promises to his disciples that if they keep his commandments, of which he has newly given them the command to love one another, then they are no longer his servants, but now his friends, *philoi* (15.14f.). This saying, reinforced by the use of *phileō* in 16.27, **'the Father himself is your friend, because you have been mine'** may well have been what emboldened George Fox to call his followers **'the Friends of the Lord'**, and to create the Religious Society of Friends.

'All friends of the Lord every where,' Fox writes, **'whose minds are turned within towards the Lord, take heed and hearken to the light within you, which is the light of Christ and of God... And the light of God... turns** (your minds) **to God, [and] to an endless being, joy and peace.'**[97]

That passage, with its words of light, eternal life, joy and peace, offers a suitably Johannine note on which to conclude.

Appendix A

The Theatre of Dionysus
at Athens

The views expressed in Chapter Three and in the Excursus about skene and ekkyklema differ from those of some of today's leading scholars, so here, to show the basis for my suggestions, I set out my own interpretation of the evidence for the development of the earliest Greek *theatron,* the first site and first building specifically designed for the performance of drama.

The theatre of Dionysus in Athens was constructed, early in the fifth century BC, to supersede the *agora* (the market-place) as the venue for the dramatic performances with which the feast of Dionysus was celebrated. Its initial construction was probably little more than a level dance floor of beaten earth or perhaps, since it was the precinct of the god, of stone paving (the orchestra), with some seating provided, mostly if not entirely of wood; and a wooden wall which served as a backdrop and screened some simple rooms behind it, to serve for changing of costume and storing of properties (the skene). Although Taplin doubts whether any such structure existed much before the middle of the fifth century,[98] I hold that the new dramatic area most probably reproduced some basic elements to which playwrights and actors would have become accustomed in the agora. The back wall (with its dressing and storage rooms behind), we may suppose, from its name, *skēnē*, which means 'tent', to have replaced some sort of small canvas marquee; which, like the wooden seats for spectators, would have been set up newly in the agora for each festival. The purpose of the 'tent' would have been primarily to be a place where costumes and masks could be stored ready, and where an actor could go to change his mask before reappearing as a different character.

The agora was surrounded with fine buildings, however, and that might have suggested a change at the new site from a mere tent to a back wall representing the façade of an important building, with a large central doorway. Such a wall, if decently done in planking and covered with a hard plaster like gypsum, could have looked well in this new theatre, while the hard coating would also have made it an effective sounding board. I suggest that the central doorway would have been garnished with a pediment above and pillars at either side, to look dignified and impressive; but these were almost certainly not built but painted on the flat wall, to *look* three dimensional rather than to be so. Quite possibly the painter – and skene-painting became a known skill and trade – would have carried his decoration across the whole façade; but the central doorway, as the focal point of the drama, would have been of prime importance. Painting would be relatively cheap, and the skene-wall could be repainted for each dramatic festival

This new skene was certainly a temporary structure in the sense that it had no foundations sunk into the bedrock of brecchia, as the later buildings had; but it seems improbable that, as has been claimed, it would have been taken down between festivals and been, therefore, a very slight structure of wood and canvas. The city would have wanted its new theatre to do it credit, and the precinct of a god required something which would enhance, rather than detract, from its dignity; and surely one advantage of the new site, as opposed to the agora, was that here the skene and the tiers of seats would *not* have to be dismantled after every Dionysian festival to make way for the resumption of daily business. To begin with, however, the skene was merely a suitably dignified backdrop, in front of which the actors, entering by the *parodoi* (side-entrances; also *eisodoi*), performed. Dramatically, the skene had no particular identity or relevance until and unless the text of the play identified it as palace, temple, city, or beetling crag.

Architectural propriety would have required that this fine facade should, like any important building, stand above several steps, probably surmounted by a plinth, all running its full length;[99] the structural needs of a free standing skene would argue for a broad plinth, to allow steady support on the forward side (See diagram). Those steps and plinth would have been all the 'stage' it had, reproducing what actors in the agora had quite probably become accustomed to using; for it is natural for anyone declaiming or singing in the open air to use any raised standpoint available, as the legend, true or not, of Thespis mounting a table (*eleos*) confirms; and the Greeks were well aware that a raised position helped the voice to carry.

Rehm contends (1994, p.36) that a low 'stage' like this would not give a better view of the actors except to the very small percentage of the audience who were not, like the majority, looking down on the performers; but this seems to ignore the fact that those lowest tiers of seats were precisely the seats of the rich and influential, on whose support the dramatic festival depended. Furthermore, even spectators higher up the hillside might see the actors and their gestures more clearly if silhouetted against the plastered skene which I have suggested, and hear them better too, than if they sang and acted at the same level with the chorus in the orchestra. Down there the chorus would have had to be placed behind them, offering a much less sharp and distinctive background than the skene; or placed to the sides of the orchestra, so obstructing the view of some of those important people in the horseshoe of best seats which ran round three sides of the dance-floor (see below).

Performance would also have demanded, not perhaps the proper dressing-rooms found in later theatres, but at least some covered area behind the wall, to serve the purposes of the original tent in the agora. Thus the wall itself would have been buttressed in front and supported behind (again, see diagram), making it able to stand firm with little, if any, foundation.[100]

I agree with Rehm (1994, p.33) that an orchestra need not always have been circular, and that the lovely proportions and circular orchestra of the much later, Hellenistic, theatre at Epidaurus have over-influenced thinking on this point. I suggest that in the original theatre of Dionysus the orchestra had straight tiers of seating flanking the dance-floor on two opposite sides, where earthen embankments had been constructed;[101] and, linking those, one side on which the tiers of seats followed the curve of the hill. On the fourth side would have been the skene, standing approximately where now a Roman wall has truncated the Hellenistic circular orchestra,[102] but leaving room either side for the vital parodoi (passages), by which first the audience and later the actors entered.

Rehm and Taplin infer from the fact that the earliest plays do not suggest entry through the central doorway, nor the use of the ekkyklema to reveal indoor scenes, that neither feature existed during the earliest phase, nor even perhaps the skene façade itself;[103] but the argument from silence is never secure. I suggest that both doorway and ekkyklema existed from the first, but that originally the ekkyklema was only required to serve as the mound, hillock, outcrop or tumulus -- usually graced with an altar, or statues of the gods, or some memorial, to represent a shrine or tomb -- which it is agreed that even some of the earliest plays do require. Further, that, apart from existing as an appropriate architectural feature of the skene façade, the original function of the central doorway was simply to house the ekkyklema and allow it to be pushed forward on the broad plinth in front of that façade as much as a particular play required.

Given that the texts of some early plays by Aeschylus do require some sort of mound,[104] an ekkyklema newly invented for this purpose seems far more practical than the permanent mound of earth, or even of rock left *in situ*, standing centrally, or to one side, just beyond the orchestra, which have been suggested. Even less practical would have been a suggested mound contrived in the centre of the orchestra, which then requires a further solution, possibly an underground passage, to allow the ghost of Darius to 'rise' and then speak from the top of his grave. If a mound was the original function of the ekkyklema, further uses such as entry and exit through the central doorway or the revealing of interior scenes, would have developed naturally later; as did using the top of the skene for a *theologeion*, where the gods might appear to address the humans below. These earliest uses of the ekkyklema would not have required the eight-foot width which later uses seem to demand.

Pickard-Cambridge rejected as '**mere superstitions and contrary to what we know of human nature and freedom**' the ideas implied by other scholars that variations in structure always take place in logical order, so that their chronological order may be inferred from that; that any structure which is found in stone must previously have existed in wood; and that '**no artist (or architect) ever thought of anything for himself**'.[105] Accepting that chronology cannot be safely be argued from a logical order, I believe that most practical, as opposed to artistic, development usually shows a logical order, being developed to meet perceived needs. But the solution to any problem may be brilliantly inventive, and while the Greek stage perhaps developed step by step, the ekkyklema was a great leap forward: a most ingenious invention, meeting a perceived need in a new way and with a huge potential for uses previously undreamed of.

Taplin's appreciation of Aeschylus' innovative use of ekkyklema and skene in the *Oresteia* trilogy suggests to me that the playwright, having originally used the ekkyklema only for such play-long features as Darius' tomb, Prometheus' rock and the Suppliant Maidens' shrine, had now perceived new ways in which the existing technology could be applied. This would be no less to the credit of the great tragedian, but surely more probable, than to suppose that he simultaneously created, at a single stroke, both the machinery *and* all its possible uses.

Appendix B

The Authorship of the Fourth Gospel

One might simply argue that if the fourth evangelist was a would-be dramatist who became a novelist, and who adapted the Synoptic gospels creatively, using a vivid imagination, then he could not have been an eyewitness, nor used an eyewitness as his source. Yet that might seem too sweeping, and the case must be set out in detail.

The evangelist's identification of his source as the beloved disciple -- and implicitly, when the church chose to take it so, as John bar Zebedee[106] -- may be rated as one of his most skilful achievements. But a novelist's pseudo-authentication of his witness is tantamount to declaring that that person was *not* the source; and for many people the nature of the miracles ascribed to Jesus in this gospel is incompatible with his source having been a truthful eyewitness.[107] For example, Jesus Walking on Water, which in Mark's version could be a simple misunderstanding by Mark of what Peter had told him, is allowed no such rational explanation by John, who has Jesus walking across from one side of the lake almost to the other. The same is true of the Jerusalem healings in John; they simply confirm that this gospel is a work of creative imagination. That being so, attempts to attribute the gospel to any disciple would be vain.

John bar Zebedee was probably martyred early, like his brother James;[108] and his connection with Ephesus and the province of Asia seems wholly imaginary, deriving only from his later identification with the beloved disciple and through him (John 21.20-24) with the long lived disciple to whom the evangelist ascribes the authorship of his book.[109] That long lived disciple, John the Elder, did at least properly belong at Ephesus. He was known to Polycarp and to Papias, both born around 70 AD, which makes plausible Irenaeus' claim that the Elder lived until the reign of Trajan (98-117). Papias, and Polycrates (bishop of Ephesus, c.190) both published lists which differentiate this disciple John from Bar Zebedee, one of the Twelve;[110] but anecdotes given by Eusebius suggest that he was a strong personality, and the term 'elder' probably relates to his having been an eyewitness to Jesus and a founding father of the Asian church. There seems no particular reason to doubt the story that he was sent to the salt-mines of Patmos; it is even conceivable that he wrote the Apocalypse attributed to him; but an eye-witness would not, surely, have written such a largely imagined narrative about Jesus. He was, however, the John whose name the fourth evangelist borrowed in order to shed lustre on his own brilliantly imaginative gospel.

The good, clear, but non-classical Greek in which this gospel is written suggests a well educated provincial;[111] the claims I have put forward for the dramatic and often theatrical nature of the narrative require an author well enough read in the great plays – not very frequently performed at this time – to venture to compose a new play; the theological content implies much thought. All these imply leisure to read and think and compose, the prerogative of those of some means and social standing. No first century Christian is known to fit the bill, the nearest being the probably Alexandrian author of the *Epistle to the Hebrews,* who writes very good Greek, with a fine rhetorical style, although with no apparent interest in drama. Halfway through the second century comes Justin Martyr, and later still Irenaeus, but not till the third century can the church show scholarly works like those of Origen and Clement of Alexandria.

Now cultured Christians of means and leisure were, in the first century, for the most part women. The reason was that any man wishing to work for the government, from consuls in the senate to clerks in the civil service or the newest recruit in the army, had to be willing, whatever their own gods, to burn a pinch of incense to the emperor now and again. Further, for the men from senatorial or knightly families, service in the army was an essential step in one's career; but the Christians were still, at this stage, following Jesus' precepts and refusing to fight. To become a Christian, therefore, meant to give up all prospects of rising in the world or fulfilling the family's expectations, and could be seen as highly unpatriotic.

On the other hand, if women became worshippers of foreign gods, that seems to have been nobody's business except their husband's. Josephus tells of Paulina, who worshipped Isis, and Fulvia, who converted to Judaism, both from the highest families (*Ant.*18.65-80 and 81-84). Both these ladies were victimised by unscrupulous persons; the husband in each case reported the outrage to the emperor, the priests of Isis were executed, and the Jews expelled from Rome in 19 AD.

When the wife of Aulus Plautius, the general who conquered Britain, was accused of following 'a foreign superstition', he made inquiry and decided for himself that she was not guilty. Domitian too may have been acting as much as head of the family as emperor when he decided to exile his niece Flavia Domitilla for **'atheism'**. Both these last two women have been claimed as Christians, but the evidence is thin and circumstantial. However, they at least show how easily the new religion could have found adherents amongst women of the upper classes.

Women were not only freer to choose their religion, they had found many new opportunities in the Hellenistic world and in the Graeco-Roman world which followed it. In the provinces particularly, women were traders, philosophers and doctors. Some were professional artists, athletes, musicians and poets. A few held office as magistrates; notably Philē of Priene (not far from Ephesus), who also designed a reservoir and aqueduct.[112]There was nothing to stop a well-off woman in the province of Asia from writing, and rewriting, a book, if she chose: the Priscilla in Acts, who is always named before her husband Aquila and whose name suggests an wellborn family, was suggested by Harnack as a possible author of *The Epistle to the Hebrews*.[113]

It is not impossible, of course, that there was a male author, with a deep interest in the Greek drama, a talented literary man who wrote good Greek and had leisure to write and rewrite at length; but if so, it is perhaps strange that a man so much better educated and more privileged than the majority of his fellow Christians should have remained quite unknown. There is a strong probability that this unknown cultured author was a well-off Christian woman, who used the male pseudonym of John, and worded her gospel so as to make that authoritative ascription seem plausible and attractive.

Appendix C

The Date of the Crucifixion

The only genuine historical detail in John, as distinct from a few broad facts like the crucifixion of Jesus of Nazareth ordered by Pontius Pilate, would seem to be John's dating of the crucifixion, not to the Passover itself, but to the day before, Nisan 14 in the Hebrew calendar. Other items sometimes taken as having biographical or historical value, such as the reference to Jesus as '**not yet fifty years old**', or to the temple as having taken forty-six years to build, have no corroboration; and suggest rather an author needing, as good lines for his play, a sweeping condemnation of Jesus' astounding claim that '**before Abraham was, I am**', or a splendidly resonant number like *tesserakonta kai hex* (forty and six). But that Jesus had been crucified on the Eve of the Passover was the well-authenticated witness of all the churches of the Roman province of Asia, in Western Turkey.

The vital evidence is a letter to the bishop of Rome from Polycrates, bishop of Ephesus, c.185 AD. After enumerating all the notable early Christians in Asia, starting with the apostle Philip, and '**John who leant on the Lord's breast**', he states '**all these kept the fourteenth day of the Passover** (*not a technically correct term, but it must mean the 14 Nisan, at Passovertide*) **according to the gospel, never swerving, but following the rule of**

the faith.' He goes on to say that he lives according to the tradition of his kinsmen, amongst whom he is the eighth bishop, '**and my kinsmen always kept the day when the people put away the yeast**',[114] which is precisely Nisan 14.

So the Christians in Asia, in such churches as those listed in *Revelation,* for example, had celebrated the days of Crucifixion and Resurrection annually, according to the Hebrew calendar, in a tradition unbroken from the time of the apostles; therefore they can hardly have been in error when they stated that the crucifixion was on Nisan 14, the eve of the Passover. For the apostles had certainly known the real date when it happened and, being Jews themselves, like the majority of those first converts in Asia, no doubt continued to keep the Passover each year.

Paul clearly implies this dating when he says that '**Christ our Paschal lamb is sacrificed for us, so let us keep the feast not with the old leaven of malice and wickedness, but with the unleavened bread of sincerity and truth** (I Cor.5.7,8), which immediately recalls '**the first day of unleavened bread, when they sacrificed the Passover lamb**' – a correct date which Mark seems simply to have attached to the wrong day in his narrative. Nisan 14 is also confirmed by a reference in the Talmud: '**Yeshua was hanged on the Eve of the Passover.**'[115] The Fourth Evangelist should be thought of as elaborating his 'Lamb of God' theme because of the known fact of the date, rather than, as sometimes suggested, altering the date to suit his theme.

The church at Rome, observing the correct *days*, Good *Friday* and Easter *Sunday*, rather than the correct Hebrew *dates*, could easily have been misled about the half-forgotten day of the month in an unfamiliar calendar; just as in this country the precise date of the Armistice in 1918 became unknown to many, once it was always celebrated on a Sunday. The expulsion of all Jews from Rome by Claudius, c.50 AD,[116] would have left a gentile church at Rome, with no great interest in Passover or the Hebrew calendar. We may note that in Rome's later dispute with the Quartodecimans ('Fourteenthers') it was not argued that the latter, led by the Asian churches, were celebrating the wrong date; but simply that it was wrong to celebrate on the dates given by the Jewish calendar at all, instead of on the correct days of the week, the crucifixion on a Friday followed by the Resurrection on a Sunday. (Quartodecimans fasted on Nisan 14 and celebrated Christ's triumph that evening, when Nisan 15, the Passover, began.) A growing hostility to all Jewish customs may be seen in the Roman church's wish to separate and differentiate Good Friday and Easter from the Passover feast.

Too little attention has been given to V. Taylor's exposition of the linguistic evidence which shows that Mark's Passion narrative consists of a pre-existent short written account into which he has inserted other episodes learnt from Peter.[117] In this Taylor shows that Mark probably confused the issue by inserting his story of the Man with a Pitcher of Water between the correct date of the Last Supper, **'the first day of unleavened bread, when they used to kill the Passover lamb'** (Mk.14.12 ; and definitely Nisan 14) and **'when evening was come he comes with the twelve'** (14.17). A gentile Christian in Rome might easily have overlooked the fact that the Hebrew date in the evening, after sunset, was not the same as the date earlier on the same (Roman) day. In other words, Mark's *source* probably gave the same dating as John does; and did not equate the Last Supper with the Passover meal. Which does not mean that the fourth evangelist has suddenly revealed an unexpected concern for fact, but merely that being, as he probably was, a Christian from Ephesus or thereabouts, he simply went by local usage in the province of Asia. That he was here correct seems a happy accident.

Short Bibliography

Greek Novel and GreekTheatre

Arnott, P.D., *Public Performance in Greek Theatre*, Routledge 1991.

Aylen, L., *The Greek Theater*, Associated University Presses, Toronto, 1985

Balmer, J., *Classical Women Poets*, Bloodaxe, Newcastle on Tyne, 1996.

Beacham, R., *'Playing Places: the temporary and the permanent',* in *The Cambridge Companion to Greek and Roman Theatre*, eds. McDonald, M., and Walton, J.M., CUP 2OO7.

Beaton, R., ed., *The Greek Novel, AD 1-1985*, Croon Helm, Beckenham, 1988.

Dihle, A., *Greek and Latin Literature of the Roman Empire*, tr. M. Malzahl, Routledge 1994.

Easterling, P.E., ed., *The Cambridge Companion to Greek Theatre*, CUP, 1997.

Green, J.R., *Theatre in Ancient Greek Society*, Routledge 1994.

Gruen, E.S., *Diaspora. Jews amidst Greeks and Romans*, Harvard UP, 2002.

Hagg, T., *The Novel in Antiquity*, Blackwell, Oxford 1983.

Holst-Warhaft, G., *Dangerous Voices. Women's Laments and Greek Literature*, first pub.1992, Routledge 1995.

Jacobson H., *The Exagogue of Ezekiel*, CUP 1983.

Jones, P.V., ed., *The World of Athens: An Introduction to Classical Athenian Culture*, CUP 1984.

Kallen, H.M., *The Book of Job as a Greek Tragedy*, Moffatt, Yard & Co, New York 1959.

Morgan J.R. and Stoneman,R. eds., *Greek Fiction. The Greek Novel in Context*, Routledge 1994.

Perry, B.E., *The Ancient Romances*, Univ. California, Berkeley, 1967.

Pickard-Cambridge, A.W., *The Theatre of Dionysus at Athens*, Clarendon, Oxford, 1946.

-----------------------------, *Dramatic Festivals of Athens*, 2nd ed., rev. by J. Gould and D.M. Lewis, OUP 1968.

Reardon, B.P., *Collected Ancient Greek Novels*, Univ. California, Berkeley 1989.

Rehm, R., *Greek Tragic Theatre*, Routledge 1994.

----------, '*The Staging of Suppliant Plays*', pp.276-83 in *Greek, Roman and Byzantine Studies* 1988.

Sifakis,, G.M., *Studies in the History of Hellenistic Drama*, Athlone Press, London, 1967.

Stoneman, R., *The Greek Alexander Romance*, Penguin Books, 1991.

Taplin, O., *The Stagecraft of Aeschylus*, first pub.1977, OUP 2001.

------------, *Greek Tragedy in Action*, Routledge 1989.

------------, '*Greek Theatre:The Pictorial Record*', pp.13-48 in *The Oxford Illustrated History of Theatre*, ed. Brown, J.R., OUP, 1995.

------------, '*The pictorial record*', pp.69-90, in *The Cambridge Companion to Greek Tragedy*, ed.P.E. Easterling. CUP 1997.

Tuilier, A., *La Pasion de Christe, Tragedie*, Sources Chretiennes No.149, Paris 1969

Walton, J.M., *Greek Theatre Practice*, rev. ed., Methuen 1991.

Webster, T.B.L., *Greek Theatre Production*, 2nd ed., Methuen 1970.

-------------------, *The Greek Chorus*, Methuen 1970.

Whitmarsh, T.J.G, *Ancient Greek Literature*, Polity Press, Cambridge, 2004.

Whitmarsh, T.J.G., ed., *The Cambridge Companion to the Greek and Roman Novel*, CUP 2008.

Wills, L.M., *The Jewish Novel in the Ancient World*, Cornell U.P., 1995.

Wilson, P., *The Athenian Institution of the Khoregia*, CUP 2000.

Wycherley, R.E., *The Stones of Athens*, Princeton U.P., 1978

The Gospel of John

Ashton, J.E., ed., *The Interpretation of John*, 2nd. ed., T. & T. Clark, Edinburgh 1997.

--------------, *Studying John*, Clarendon Press, Oxford 1994.

Barrett, C.K., *Jesus and the Gospel Tradition*, SPCK 1967.

---------------, *New Testament Essays*, SPCK 1972.

---------------, *The Gospel according to St John*, 2nd ed. SPCK 1978.

Bauckham, R., *Jesus and the Eyewitnesses*, Eerdmanns, Grand Rapids USA, 2006.

----------------, *The Testimony of the Beloved Disciple*, Baker Academic, Grand Rapids, USA, 2007.

Blomberg, C.L., *The Historical Reliability of John's Gospel*, IVF Press, Leicester 2001.

Brown, R.E., *New Testament Essays*, Chapman, London, 1965

Bruce, F.F., '*The Trial of Jesus in the Fourth Gospel*', in *Gospel Perspectives, Vol.1*, eds. France, E.T. and Wenham, D., J.S.O.T. Press, Sheffield, 1980.

Bultmann, R., *The Gospel of John. A Commentary*, tr. G.R.B. Murray et al., OUP 1971.

Burge, G.M., *Interpreting the Gospel of John*, Baker Books, Grand Rapids, USA, 1992.

Culpepper, R.A., *The Anatomy of the Fourth Gospel*, Fortress Press, Philadelphia, 1983.

--------------------, *John, the Son of Zebedee*, T&T. Clark, Edinburgh, 2000.

Davies, M., *Rhetoric and Reference in the Fourth Gospel*, Sheffield Academic Press, 1992.

Dodd, C.H., *The Interpretation of the Fourth Gospel*, CUP, 1953.

--------------, *Historical Tradition in the Fourth Gospel*, CUP, 1963.

Fortna, R.T., *The Gospel of Signs. A Reconstruction of the Narrative Source underlying the Fourth Gospel*, CUP 1970.

--------------, *The Fourth Gospel and its Predecessor*, T&T Clark, Edinburgh 1988.

Funk, R.W., Hoover R. and the Jesus Seminar, *The Five Gospels*, Scribner New York 1996.

Hanson, A.T., *The Prophetic Gospel*, T&T. Clark, 1991.

Hengel, M., *The Johannine Question*, tr.J. Bowden, SCM Press 1989

Johnson, L.T., *The Real Jesus*, HarperCollins, San Francisco, 1996.

Kysar, R., *The Fourth Evangelist and his Gospel*, Augsburg Publishing, Minneapolis, 1975.

-----------, *John, The Maverick Gospel*, John Knox Press, Atlanta, 1976.

-----------, *John's Story of Jesus*, Fortress Press, Philadelphia, 1984.

Lightfoot, R.H., *St. John's Gospel. A Commentary*, Clarendon Press, Oxford 1956.

Lindars, B., *Behind the Fourth Gospel*, SPCK 1971.

-------------, *Jesus Son of Man*, SPCK 1983.

Martyn, J.L., *History and Theology in the Fourth Gospel*, Harper & Row, N.Y, 1968.

Nicol,W., *The Semeia in the Fourth Gospel – Tradition and Redaction*, Leiden, 1972.

Roberts, C.H., *An Unpublished Fragment of the Fourth Gospel in the John Rylands Library*, Manchester U.P. 1935.

Robinson, J.A.T., *The Priority of John*, SCM Press 1985.

Smalley, S.S., *John, Evangelist and Interpreter*, Paternoster Press, Exeter 1978.

Smith, D. Moody, *John among the Gospels*, Augsburg Fortress Press, Minneapolis 1992.

--------------------, *The Theology of John*, CUP, 1995.

Stibbe, M.W.G., *John. Readings. A New Biblical Commentary*, Sheffield Academic Press, 1993.

------------------, *John as Storyteller: Narrative Criticism and the Fourth Gospel*, CUP 1992.

------------------, *John's Gospel*, Routledge 1994.

Taylor, V., *The Gospel according to St. Mark*, Macmillan 1953.

Tuckett, C., ed., *The Messianic Secret*, SPCK 1983.

Westermann, C., *The Gospel of John in the Light of the Old Testament*, tr.S.S. Schatzmann, Henderson Publishers, Peabody, Mass. USA, 1998

Wills, L.M., *The Quest for the Historical Gospel*, Routledge 1997.

Winter, P., *On the Trial of Jesus*, Verlag Walter de Gruyter & Co, Berlin, 1961.

General

Barton, S. ed., *The Cambridge Companion to the Gospels*, CUP 2006.

Bockmuehl, M., ed., *The Cambridge Companion to Jesus*, CUP, 2001.

Borg, M.J., *Jesus*, HarperCollins, New York, 2006.

Boulton, D., *Who on Earth was Jesus?*, O Books, John Hunt Publishing, Ropley, 2008.

Brandon, S.G.F., *The Trial Of Jesus of Nazareth*, Batsford 1968.

Burridge, R., *What are the Gospels?*, CUP 1992.

Dillistone, F.W., *The Novelist and the Passion Story*, Collins 1960.

Duchesne,L.H., *Christian Worship, Its Origin and Evolution*, first tr. pub. 1903, 5th ed. SPCK 1956.

Dunn, J.D.G., '*The Messianic Secret in Mark*' in *The Messianic Secret*, ed. C. Tuckett, SPCK 1983.

Fox, R.L., *Pagans and Christians*, Penguin Books 1988.

Fuller, R.H., *The Formation of the Resurrection Narratives*, rev. ed. SPCK 1980.

Funk, R.W., *Language, Hermeneutic and Word of God*. Harper Row, New York 1966.

Grant, M., *Jesus*, first pub. 1977, Orion 2004.

Harvey, A.E., *Companion to the Gospels*, OUP/CUP 1972.

---------------, *Jesus and the Constraints of History*, Duckworth 1982.

James, W., *The Varieties of Religious Experience*, first pub.1902, Fontana 1960.

Legat, M., *Writing for Pleasure and Profit*, 2nd ed., Hale, 1993.

Lēgrasse, S., *The Trial of Jesus*, tr. J. Bowden, SCM Press 1997.

Lord, A.B., *The Singer of Tales*, Harvard U.P. 1960.

Pomeroy, S.B., *Goddesses, Whores, Wives and Slaves*, Pimlico 1975

Sayers, D.L., *The Man Born to be King*, Gollancz 1943

Schonfield, H.J., *The Passover Plot*, Hutchinson 1965.

Shelton, J-A., *As the Romans Did*, OUP 1988.

Stanton, G., *The Gospels and Jesus*, 2nd ed. OUP 2002 [1st 1989].

Vermes, G., *The Changing Faces of Jesus*, Penguin Books 2000.

Notes

¹ I use John to refer to the Fourth Evangelist or to his gospel whenever convenient and unambiguous. Others Johns are identified as Bar Zebedee, the Elder or the Baptist.

² Eusebius, *Ecclesiastical History*, 6.14.7. There is an earlier mention of this gospel by Irenaeus saying that he knew Christians who did not accept John as a true gospel; possibly Clement is responding to similar attitudes in Alexandria.

Chapter One

³ Lewis, *'Modern Theology and Biblical Criticism'* in *Christian Reflections*, ed. W. Hooper, Grand Rapids USA, 1967, p.211f.)

⁴ A great many *episodes* in John are very far from realistic, as will be shown.

⁵ In *Appendix A* I suggest 100-115AD as likely dating for John. Xenophon's *Ephesian Story*, Antonius Diogenes' *Wonders beyond Thule*, Lucian's *True Story*, Pseudo-Lucian's *The Ass*, Iamblichus' *Babylonian Story*, *Leucippe and Clitophon* by Achilles Tatius and *Daphnis and Chloe* by 'Longus' probably all date 100-200AD (Reardon 1989, pp.1-15).

⁶ R. Stoneman, *'The Alexander Romance: From History to Fiction'* in *Greek Fiction*, Morgan and Stoneman, 1994, p.122.

7   L.M. Wills, '*The Jewish Novellas*', in *Greek Fiction,* ed. Morgan and Stoneman, 1994.

8   However, the preservation of the heroine's virtue is mandatory in Greek novels also, and achieved even more remarkably for Tarsia, in *Pericles, Prince of Tyre*, than for the apocryphal Judith.

9   To accept this as fiction absolves the real Jesus of ordering blatant Sabbath breaking (John 8.5). Such behaviour must be the author's invention, since it could readily have led to Jesus' rapid condemnation; but the author is writing after the schism between church and synagogue, c.90AD.

10 Whitmarsh 2004, p.156: '**Because of the particular narrative form adopted in most of the Greek novels – external 'omniscient' narration – readers can access the deepest thoughts of characters, even when those characters are attempting to disguise them**'.

11 Whereas C.K. Barrett holds that some passages of John are taken from Mark, R. Kysar, M. Stibbe, D. Moody Smith and L. Wills affirm the contrary.

12 A century later Origen was provided with '**seven shorthand writers (...) no fewer copyists, and also girls well trained in writing**' (Eusebius, *EH*.6.23.2).

13 Different hypothetical sources for John are advanced in Dodd 1963, Bultmann 1963, Fortna 1970, Lindars 1971, Koester 1982, Crossan 1991, Stibbe 1992, Wills 1997.

14 C.K. Barrett, 1978, pp.271-281, pp.523-529.

15 Wills (1997, p.83) has Jesus accompany the man until the servants meet them; but that is not in the text.

[16] In Morgan & Stoneman 1994, pp.185f. E. Bowie gives instances from five ancient Greek authors.

[17] 'We' here must mean those who know the long-lived disciple now; not, as in John 1.14-16, those who knew Jesus during his earthly life; but such a shift of narrator, or corroborator, is common in Greek novels; Plato's *Symposium* is the stock example. (See T. Whitmarsh, *'Narrative'*, in Whitmarsh 2008, pp. 237-24.)

[18] Hengel (1989, pp.125-9) considers that there is deliberate ambiguity about which John is meant; Bauckham (2007, pp.73-8) discounts the reference to the Zebedees, points to two unnamed disciples, and insists on John the Elder for his Beloved Disciple.

[19] See Barrett 1978, pp.581f.

[20] Hagg 1980 corroborates many points made in this chapter: about endings, p.14; dialogue p.16; background, p.19; wonders,p.70; use of sources, p.115.

Chapter Two

[21] Jesus' family, too, are arbitrarily placed, in Cana or Capernaum or Jerusalem, wherever it suits the author. In the Synoptics (Matthew, Mark and Luke) there is no mention of Cana and the family lives at Nazareth, only visitng Capernaum in a vain attempt to persuade Jesus to come home; in John, although the name Jesus of Nazareth is used, Nazareth itself is never visited.

[22] Josephus, *Jewish War* 2.232 ; *Jewish Antiquities* 20.118. Both had probably been published before 95AD.

[23] *Tesserakonta kai hex* (46) makes a fine, resounding number, but should not be taken as fact. The temple proper was finished in 18 months, according to Josephus (*Ant*.15..421), its outer courtyards 8 years later.

[24] Evasions, 5.13, 6.15, 10.40, 11.54, 12.36; stoning, 8.59; 10.31, 39; journeys, 7.1-11; 10.41-11.16; signal,13.23-30. Cf. Whitmarsh 2004, p.157: '**Ruses and subterfuges drive novelistic narrative...**'

[25] Similarly, Mark has corrupted the dating of the Last Supper by his insertion of the Man with the Pitcher of Water story (Mark 14.12b-16) into an original Passion document; see V. Taylor 1952, (*Add. Notes J*), pp.653-664.

[26] Where, as the author knew from Mark 3.22, 7.1, critics from Judaea had sometimes appeared.

[27] The Greek of 4.54 must be read thus, since 2.23 has already alluded to signs in a Jerusalem context.

Chapter Three

[28] Sozomen, *Ecclesiastical History* 5.18; cf. also Socrates Scholasticus, *Ecclesiastical History*, 3.16; in *Nicene and Post Nicene Fathers, Vol. II*, Second Series, Eerdmans, Grand Rapids, Michigan, 1957.

[29] Although the Authorised Version also uses 'hypocrite' for Hebrew '*chanegah*', profane, it seems likely that Aramaic had adopted the Greek word for 'actor', having, like Hebrew, no term of its own for this.

[30] See particularly Oliver Taplin, *The Stagecraft of Aeschylus*, 2008, for suggested alterations in the plays of Aeschylus.

[31] Ionia, the 'Purple Land' (from the colour of its hills) had been colonised from the Greek mainland centuries before Greek theatre started.

[32] A.W. Pickard-Cambridge 1968, p.318; see also P.E. Easterling, '*From repertoire to canon*', pp.211-227 in Easterling, CUP, 1997. Plutarch witnessed the traditional celebration at Athens in 96 AD.

[33] Although some leading scholars do not believe that there was, at first, any form of stage.

[34] As in a recent production by the Welsh National Opera company. Another WNO production, of Gluck's *Iphigenie,* showed a band of invaders similarly using a forward-and-back dance-step to mime aggressiveness.

[35] The view I put forward is basically that of G.M. Walton, in his *Greek Theatre Practice*, rev. ed., 1998.

[36] Found in a mosaic of Dioscorides in the 'Villa di Cicerone' at Pompeii; see Pickard-Cambridge 1946, fig.86.

[37] I suggest a firmly fixed ladder of *flat* treads (as in an open stair or step-ladder), which, without having to protrude above the theologeion, can yet be mounted with dignity and grace by gods, or scrambled up, suggesting difficulty and effort, as here; and again in Euripides' *Phoenician Women,* ll.100-106, where Antigone needs the assistance of a slave to reach the 'roof' from a ladder. (In real life, such a ladder, fixed, often made an open stairway from the ground floor of a modest house to its upper storey.

[38] See Appendix A for further discussion of this point.

Excursus – The Ekkyklema

[39] It would be possible to hang or erect something to divide the central doorway into two, but such realism was probably not sought. The action never requires the doubleness of the cave, so the repeated references to the cave as '**double-doored**' (1.159) and '**double-gated**'(1.952) are clearly there to assist the audience to sustain this makebelieve.

[40] The chorus of suppliants might be grouped round the altar which stood in the orchestra, as Rehm supposes, and if they are kneeling Adrastus might be sufficiently visible when merely lying on a stage; but hardly, as Rehm also supposes, with neither ekkyklema nor stage.

[41] For the purposes of this study, the much debated authenticity, or not, of some passages in Aeschylus is irrelevant.

[42] Rehm suggests that the bodies might be carried out by slaves and, since he disallows the stage, laid on the ground. Would not this leave them out of sight for many people, behind the protesting chorus, and so weaken the spectacle of the triumphant Clytemnestra, gloating over her victims?

[43] The Greek bath was a shallow, flat bottomed, circular bowl, with sides about eight or nine inches high.

[44] Taplin is probably correct in suggesting that extras were used here, not dummies.

[45] She has just expressed the hope that, having killed Agamemnon, she will now be able to exorcise '**from this dwelling**' the evil spirit which has brought such harm on the descendants of Atreus.

46 J.M. Walton, *Greek Theatre Practice*, p.113, infers from the opening line of the chorus ('I come, sent out from the house'), Electra's invocation of the spirits 'that watch over my father's house' and the later concern of the chorus lest Orestes and Electra should be overheard, that the whole play takes place outside the palace; but none of these necessarily imply as much.

47 H. Weir Smyth, translator, stage direction inserted on p.245, Loeb Edition, 1922.

48 Again, I follow Taplin in letting Hermes, who never speaks, be only an invisible presence, invoked by his brother Apollo to guide Orestes on his way.

49 In a 'romance' by Achilles Tatius, (*Leucippe and Clitophon*, paras.20,21) a dagger with a retractable blade, taken from an actor's baggage, is employed; but, as described, it might not work when fixed upright, and for a suicide the actor might better fall, apparently transfixed, with his body just in front of the vertical blade, his arm just beyond it.

50 There is a cup in the J. Paul Getty Museum which shows Tecmessa holding in both hands her cloak, spread wide in front of her.

Chapter Four

51 These examples are all from Euripides (*Hecuba, Iphigenia at Aulis, The Children of Heracles*); the name Macaria is found in the legend, although no name is used in the play. Menoiceus in Euripides' *Phoenician Women* is the closest male parallel; yet he does not go tamely, but slays himself dramatically above the deadly serpent's enclosure.

52 For further parallels with *The Bacchae*, see Stibbe 1992 121-147; but he holds all these to be **'unconscious echoes'**, not **'direct literary dependence'** on Euripides' text.

53 The other two Maries would have served no purpose in a play, but have probably been reintroduced in the novel to conform with the traditional group of three women.

54 Cf. Barrett 1978, p.551 n.25. For the contrary position, Robinson 1985, p.279; but his Talmud examples are unrealistic hypothetical situations, devised merely to argue fine points of law.

55 That this ending is probably not by Aeschylus himself makes no difference here.

Chapter Five

56 Tertullian, *De Spectaculis, 26.*

57 Although at the turn of the first century there were few Christian *men* with the necessary education and leisure, there were many more such women. The author of Hebrews, whether male or, as Harnack suggested, female, displays a good standard of education.

Possibly as early as the fourth century, *Christus Patiens,* a play on the Passion of Christ, was put together with lines taken from the classical tragedies, especially from Euripides' *Bacchae* (Tuilier 1969, pp.73f).

58 There is a survey of previous scholarship on the fictive and tragic nature of John in Stibbe 1992, pp.121-129.

59 Polyneices, the rebel, is brought into the city by his mother to meet his usurping brother before the battle; later, they

slay each other in single combat. Creon has been given a second son, Menoiceus, to be an example of unselfish loyalty. Antigone repudiates her betrothal to Creon's elder son and can only embrace, not bury, the body of Polyneices, before leaving Thebes to lead Oedipus to Colonos.

[60] Canon John Davies, drawing this to my attention, also points out that one can easily reconstruct the play from the novel.

[61] Transmuting water into wine could hardly be staged convincingly, and would more probably evoke derision; The discussion with the woman at the well lacks drama, and the whole story needs constant changes of place.

Chapter Six

[62] One important scene is now located at Bethany, but the author stresses how close that is to Jerusalem (John 11.18). Similarly, in *Ajax*, set outside Troy, Sophocles has Athena state that the Greek hero's tent is the one at the far end of the line, so that the location can shift easily from there to the lonely beach.

[63] E.g., in the penultimate scene of Lope de Vega's *Caballero de Olmedo,* where a delightful family scene leads us to forget for the moment that the hero has already been murdered in the scene before.

[64] Had the missing plays of the *Prometheus* trilogy survived, we would have a cosmic plot for comparison.

[65] Following a terrible and gruesome siege, Jerusalem was captured by Titus, the temple despoiled and destroyed, much of the city razed and many of its surviving inhabitants enslaved.

Chapter Seven

[66] Luke's lepers (17.14f.) are healed as they go, but clearly before they have gone far. The centurion's slave and the Syro-Phoenician woman's daughter are not sent away, for they have never been brought to Jesus.

[67] Dionysus has a special mask which lets Pentheus crop his hair. Since stage knives with retractable blades were known, so adjustable 'eye-lids' would be possible.

[68] **'They took his clothes and divided them into four, one part for each soldier'** (Jn.20.23a).

[69] The brilliantly shining robes of the goddess in a recent production of Gluck's *Iphigenie en Tauride* showed how useful that convention still is in the theatre.

[70] **'A great many of the appeals, commands and questions expressed by one character to another or to the chorus also function as cues to the audience.'** (Easterling 1997, p.158.)

[71] For a clear discussion of this point, see pp.152f. of Easterling, 'Form and Performance', in Easterling 1997.

[72] In Aeschylus' *Libation Bearers* Pylades has a single, but important, line; which is probably spoken by a fourth person, who might therefore qualify as an actor, but was probably simply an extra with a good speaking voice.

[73] Stibbe 1994, p.106, citing others also.

[74] Compared with ten in Mark. John has three all in a single Galilean incident (6.67-71); the fourth, in a sentence linking

the *two* indoor resurrection appearances of the narrative version, identifies Thomas Didymus as '**one of the Twelve**'; perhaps a hint that he should therefore have been more ready to believe.

Chapter Eight

[75] The first stages of the schism are charted, from the Christian point of view, in Acts.

[76] The re-writing of the twelfth of the Eighteen Benedictions, c.85-90 AD, specifically named the Nazarenes as persons to be rejected by God and men. See Barrett 1978, pp.361-2, note to John 9.22.

[77] Somewhat similar is the use in English of 'Holland' to apply to the whole of the Netherlands, of which Holland is only one region.

[78] The dramatist would dress his chorus in appropriate masks and costumes (old men, young warriors, Bacchic maenads, respectable women etc.) and let their words identify them as precisely as required; and if the chorus for the play were to be, as so often, the local inhabitants, this would seem so natural to an audience that the chorus might never be named on stage at all. *Hierosolumitai* might only have appeared in a list of the cast.

[79] In many cases the title of the play is simply the name of the chorus, e.g. Troiades, the Women of Troy; but where this is not so, the identity of the chorus can usually only be inferred from the text.

80 Even Pilate's phrase 'King of the Jews' as equivalent to Messiah would make perfect sense as 'King of Jerusalem', or at least of Judaea; for Pilate's responsibility went no further.

81 Caiaphas also uses *ho laos*, the people, in this sense.

82 Stated in precisely those words in John 7.13, 19.38, and 20.19; and in different phrasing in 7.1, 9.22 and 11.54.

83 See Ashton, *Studying John: Approaches to the Fourth Gospel*, 1998, pp.36-70, for a detailed study of this point.

84 In the Sanhedrin, however, the Pharisees had a large representation, probably a majority.

85 The little we know about the costumes used for choruses in classical tragedy nowhere mentions difference of dress; yet when, as in Euripides' *Suppliant Women*, the mothers of the seven dead heroes should be no more than seven at most, with the remainder of the chorus as their attendants, some such difference might be expected; still more so if the sons of the heroes in fact formed part of the same fifteen-member chorus, with just two attendants and the historically correct six surviving mothers, which seems to me a possibility. Little Hellenistic drama survives, but the fragments preserved of the *Exagoge* by Ezekiel seem to suggest a chorus differently garbed for successive acts.

86 The chorus most often are not present right at the beginning, but enter soon after.

Chapter Nine

[87] The increased height of the Hellenistic stage makes it unlikely that the chorus would ever come up onto the stage; although a production of Aeschylus' *Eumenides* might still see them enter from the central door and later descend to the orchestra.

[88] A Pompeian mosaic illustrates such a scene (from comedy) on the ekkylema (Pickard-Cambridge 1946, fig.95).

[89] In John 18.1 it is merely 'a garden'.

[90] The judge's seat was such an integral part of the administration of justice that Herod Philip, tetrarch of Iturea and Trachonitis, always took a portable throne when touring his wild territories, so that he could deal with cases on the spot (Josephus, *Ant*.18.107).

Chapter Ten

[91] **'Who, although in the form of god (*morphē theou*), did not think being the same as god was something to cling onto'** Phil.2.6

[92] Neither Mt.11.2-6 nor Lk.7.18-23 suggests disciples transferring their allegiance. The group who have been baptised as followers of the Baptist's way, discovered by Paul at Ephesus c.53 AD, who then accept baptism in the name of Jesus (Acts 19.2-7), are not relevant to discipleship in Jesus' lifetime.

[93] *Theos,* divine, but not *ho theos*, God. See Harvey 1982, *App.3.*

94 Jephthah's daughter, betrayed by ill luck but accepting her fate bravely and obediently (Judges 11.30-40) is as moving as any similar heroine in Euripides.

95 Mark records Jesus as telling the disciples that when arraigned, as they would be, before '**governors and kings**', they were not to worry beforehand about what they should say, '**but say whatever is given to you in that hour, for it is not you who are speaking but the Holy Spirit**' (Mk.13.11). John has considerably amplified that instruction, but always in terms of the experience of the early church.

96 Beth Allen, quoted in *Quaker Faith and Practice*, British Yearly Meeting 1995, Ch.10, entry 28.

97 Fox, Epistle 56 (1653), *Works* 7:71f.; cited by Rex Ambler, *Truth of the Heart*, Quaker Books 2001, Part 1, entry 59, p.24. It is often supposed that Quakers began as 'Friends of the Truth', but here there is definite evidence for 'Friends of the Lord'.

Appendix A

98 R. Rehm, *Greek Tragic Theatre*, Routledge 1994, p.34; O. Taplin, *The Stagecraft of Aeschylus*, OUP 2001, pp.454f.

99 A possibility envisaged by A.W. Pickard-Cambridge, *The Theatre of Dionysus at Athens*, Clarendon Press, Oxford 1946, p.74, note: '**All that seems to be required in the fifth century is the provision (in certain plays) of one or two broad steps supporting (e.g.) an altar, or of *the steps which would naturally form the basis of a temple or palace* – in other words, *the basis of the scenae frons*' (my

italics). I suggest that if these steps were regarded simply as an integral part of the façade, that would account for there being no separate word for 'stage' in the Greek terminology of the early period.

[100] Its timbers may have sunk, or been sunk, into such soil as there may have been above the bedrock then, but that could only have been a matter of inches; enough perhaps to prevent it shifting easily, but certainly not the deep postholes required by a free-standing wall.

[101] It seems likely that in the agora the spectators had been accommodated in three straight banks of seating, defining three sides of a rectangular orchestra, since that would have been the easiest and most practical arrangement for the tiers of seats.

[102] See Pickard-Cambridge, *The Theatre of Dionysus*, 1946, frontispiece and Plan 1. Richard Beacham's suggestion (Beacham 2007) that the precinct floor was originally circular, but then truncated by the skene in order that the skene too could stand within that defined precinct, may well be true; but the resulting position of the skene would have been the same.

[103] Rehm, *Greek Tragic Theatre*, pp.33-35 allows the skene as façade, with central doorway, but no stage, however low; Taplin, also ruling out any low wooden stage, doubts the skene itself in the earliest phase (*The Stagecraft of Aeschylus*, p.454 n.1) and even the central door until the introduction of the ekkyklema (*TSOA,* p.455 n.1), which he supposes was first used in Aeschylus' mid fifth century Oresteia trilogy.

[104] See Excursus above. *The Persians* (472 BC) requires '**the tomb's high crest**'; *Suppliant Maidens*, (c.463?) an altar on the '**hillock**' which Danaus uses later as a lookout post; *Prometheus Bound* (date unknown) a rock to whose '**high summit**' he is nailed.

[105] Pickard-Cambridge, *The Theatre of Dionysus*, Introduction, p. vii. A fourth point was '**that careless work in stone is only possible in late periods**', but that is not relevant here.

Appendix B

[106] See in Chapter Two, '*Fictitious Sources', 'Closing the Story'*.

[107] My own objection is to the moral aspect of miracles serving relatively trivial ends, while the deity appears to ignore appalling evils. I accept the reality of some non-medical healings, but not in such cases as John describes.

[108] Hengel has made out a strong case (*The Johannine Question*, 1989, p.20 and n.121), for accepting the report of John bar Zebedee's early martyrdom from Philip of Side, who claimed Papias as his source, R.A. Culpepper (2000, pp.170-174) gives a balanced review of all sources.

[109] Supported later not only by the church but by the tourist industry, ancient and modern. I have been shown the house in Ephesus "**which John shared with Jesus' mother**".

[110] Papias, having listed a John among six other members of the Twelve, then comes to Aristion and John, '**disciples of the Lord**'; Polycrates, in a list of leading lights of the Asian church, puts '**Philip, one of the twelve apostles**' in first place, together with his daughters. Then '**there is John, too,**

who lay on the Lord's breast and was a priest wearing the petalon (breastplate) **and a martyr and a teacher. He sleeps at Ephesus**'. ('Lay on the Lord's breast' derives from the Fourth Gospel, the priest and petalon remain a puzzle.)

[111] See C.K. Barrett, *The Gospel according to St John*, 2nd ed. SPCK 1978, pp.5-11.

[112] See S.B. Pomeroy, *Goddesses, Whores, Wives and Slaves*, Pimlico, London, 1996, pp.120-141; also J. Balmer, *Classical Women Poets*, Blooodaxe, Newcastle-on-Tyne, 1996.

[113] Cited by F. Narborough, *The Epistle to the Hebrews*, Clarendon 1930, p.12.

Appendix C

[114] Polycrates, bishop of Ephesus, writing c.185AD (Eusebius, *EH* 5.24.2-7). He speaks only for his own province, but the Quartodeciman usage seems to have been that of most or all of the Near East.

[115] Babylonian Talmud, *Sanhedrin* 43.

[116] Suetonius asserts that this was never completed; but if, as he also says, the reason was strife between Jews and Christians, the removal of all Jews who were Christians was probably given priority. Normally, until the Jewish War, the traditional Jew was *persona grata* in Rome.

[117] *The Gospel according to St. Mark*, 1953, *Additional Notes J*, (pp.653-664, esp. p.660), and *K*, (pp.664-667).